THINKING
&
SINGING

Brian Bartlett
Robert Bringhurst
Dennis Lee
Tim Lilburn
Don McKay
Jan Zwicky

Thinking and Singing

Poetry and the Practice of Philosophy

Robert Bringhurst · Dennis Lee
Tim Lilburn · Don McKay · Jan Zwicky

Edited by Tim Lilburn

with an introduction by Brian Bartlett

CORMORANT BOOKS

Preface, Philosophical Apokatastasis and *Going Home*, copyright © 2002 by Tim Lilburn. *Introduction*, copyright © 2002 by Brian Bartlett. *Body Music*, copyright © 1998, 2002 by Dennis Lee. *The Bushtits' Nest*, copyright © 2001, 2002 by Don McKay. *The Philosophy of Poetry and the Trashing of Doctor Empedokles* and *Poetry and Thinking*, copyright © 2002 by Robert Bringhurst. *Dream Logic* and *Once Upon a Time in the West*, copyright © 1999, 2002 by Jan Zwicky.

All rights reserved. The use of any part of this publication, reproduced, transmitted in any form or by any means, electronic, mechanical, photocopying, recording, or stored in a retrieval system, or otherwise, without the prior consent of the publisher – or, in case of photocopying or other reprographic copying, without a licence from Cancopy (Canadian Copyright Licensing Agency) – is an infringement of the copyright law.

The publisher gratefully acknowledges the support of the Canada Council for the Arts and the Ontario Arts Council for its publishing program. We acknowledge the financial support of the Government of Canada through the Book Publishing Industry Development Program (BPIDP) for our publishing activities.

Printed and bound in Canada

National Library of Canada Cataloguing in Publication Data

    Main entry under title:
      Thinking and Singing

    ISBN 1-896951-38-4

    1. Poetry. 2. Philosophy. 3. Literature – Philosophy.
    I. Lilburn, Tim, 1950–

    PN1064.T48 2002   809.1   C2002-900041-6

Cover concept: Tannice Goddard
Cover photo: copyright © 2002 by Dolores Pitcher
Typography: Robert Bringhurst

CORMORANT BOOKS INC.
62 Rose Avenue
Toronto, Ontario, Canada M4X 1N9
www.cormorantbooks.com

Contents

1 *Preface* · Tim Lilburn
5 *Introduction: Two Pianos Together* · Brian Bartlett

PART ONE

19 *Body Music: Notes on Rhythm in Poetry* · Dennis Lee
59 *The Bushtits' Nest* · Don McKay
79 *The Philosophy of Poetry and the Trashing of Doctor Empedokles* · Robert Bringhurst
95 *Philosophical Apokatastasis: On Writing and Return* · Tim Lilburn
121 *Dream Logic and the Politics of Interpretation* · Jan Zwicky

PART TWO

155 *Poetry and Thinking* · Robert Bringhurst
173 *Going Home* · Tim Lilburn
187 *Once Upon a Time in the West: Heidegger and the Poets* · Jan Zwicky

201 *Notes on Contributors*

ACKNOWLEDGEMENTS

Dennis Lee's "Body Music: Notes on Rhythm in Poetry" is reprinted with permission, and with the author's latest revisions, from his book of essays *Body Music* (House of Anansi Press, Toronto, 1998).

Don McKay's "The Bushtits' Nest" is reprinted with permission from his book *Vis à Vis* (Gaspereau Press, Wolfville, Nova Scotia, 2001).

A preliminary version of Robert Bringhurst's "The Philosophy of Poetry and the Trashing of Doctor Empedokles" appeared as "Postscript to a Translation of Empedocles," *The Ohio Review* 16.3 (Spring 1975).

A version of Jan Zwicky's "Dream Logic and the Politics of Interpretation" appeared as "Freud's Metapsychology and the Culture of Philosophy" in *Civilization and Oppression,* edited by Catherine Wilson (*Canadian Journal of Philosophy* Supplementary Volume 25, 1999).

Robert Bringhurst's "Poetry and Thinking" is the text of a lecture commissioned by Luther College in the University of Regina, delivered there in January 2001.

Preface

I WROTE TO TEN POETS a few years ago, asking them to think about two questions – what does poetry know and how does it know? – and to write about what these questions suggested to them. Their essays were published in *Poetry and Knowing* in 1995, but the questions themselves carried on; it didn't occur to me to stop asking them. They first had appeared in conversations I had been having with Don McKay and Jan Zwicky that began in the late 1980s when I was living with them while I was writer-in-residence at the University of Western Ontario; these talks took place over kitchen tables first at Coldstream, in that winter of 1989, then at Batchawana Bay, later in the Moosewood Sandhills, Fredericton, Saskatoon, Mayerthorpe, Edmonton, Victoria: they would begin at breakfast and often carry through until lunch. In the early days, I was reading Dennis Lee and Robert Bringhurst for the first time; Jan Zwicky was in correspondence with Bringhurst. It seemed to me that I was engaged in a five-pointed conversation, even though some of the participants spoke chiefly from the page; it kept turning up new things and pushing along in a rough direction.

The hunch slowly grew in me that poetry was a particular form of knowing that dominant, current thinking – contemporary philosophy, economics, sociology, psychology – didn't know or had forgotten. Later, after *Poetry and Knowing,* I began to believe that poetry was a way of doing philosophy, perhaps was the true way or a residual version of this, though I realized that most professional philosophers would find this claim heterodox.

Poetry and long talk: oddly, in effect, the two appear equivalent: both are beckoning ways in; both are maieutic, lifting to the tongue latent things, lit things no one planned to say. Neither, it seems, fully trusts its elder brother, systematic thought; each will upend it; sometimes, however, poetry or dialectic will use system to draw what needs saying further along. It can seem with such talk that the conversation itself often is doing the thinking, the speakers contributing simply their confusion, their pressing to know, each listening for where the talk wants to go, attempting to "hear" the watercourse it's found. Many poets say that poetry, too, is largely listening, that what is wanted is a kind of negative attention, an alert emptiness – Osip Mandelstam cocking his ear as he composed. This book is not the unravelling of a single thought; there is disagreement in what follows – not all believe Plato is saying something interesting, for instance; not all are caught by the ontological possibilities in poetry's music. Nor is anyone laying down any program in *Thinking and Singing*; there is no position or technique – where language comes closest to real estate – just the drift of rumination: all the writing has an open ear, proceeds by this ear: a certain form of speech can be an attempt to hear. Writing like this, I believe, harbours a kind of politics – antipodal to management – that grows from alacritous attention.

So the conversation goes on, over food, on the telephone, on the page; others join in; the dead frequently interrupt and direct the flow. Martin Heidegger, of course, is present for good or ill; Plato is here; Emmanuel Levinas is here; the many thinkers and contemplatives within the Dionysian strand of the Christian contemplative tradition; the pre-Socratics; Ludwig Wittgenstein; Sigmund Freud; Simone Weil; George Grant: come in; lunch is made; tea is poured: tell me what you've been thinking; tell me what you really think. It's a long meal, with many hiatuses, that no one has thought to end; people are free to come and go as they please. You are welcome to join in; pull up a chair, lean back from the table. Where were we?

¶ Talk among those who don't quite know, but who have the scent of what they wish to know in their noses, who are exercised, reaching, is a remarkably flexible instrument, capable of getting into places that offer no tool room to argument, to writing, even to imagination. Because of this capacity to surprise, because its fruits are both apt and peculiar, talk like this can be nothing other than daimonic: and for such visitations one can only feel gratitude. I wish to thank all in this book for the treasure of their thought and conversation over the years. I wish also to thank Marc Côté and Sue Stewart of Cormorant Books for their enthusiasm without which *Thinking and Singing: Poetry and the Practice of Philosophy* would not exist as a volume.

TIM LILBURN

Brian Bartlett

Introduction:
Two Pianos Together

IN "THE RAVEN AND THE FIRST MEN," a Haida tale told by Bill Reid and Robert Bringhurst, the human race emerges this way:

At first [the Raven] saw nothing, but as he scanned the beach again, a white flash caught his eye, and when he landed he found at his feet, half buried in the sand, a gigantic clamshell. When he looked more closely still, he saw the shell was full of little creatures cowering in terror of his enormous shadow.
  Well, here was something to break the monotony of his day....

As someone raised in a culture that has shaped images of *Homo sapiens* as the triumph of creation, the apex of evolution, a creature fallen but made in the image of God, I laughed when I first read this the other day while riding on Calgary's LRT (Light Rapid Transit). I'd just bought a copy of *The Raven Steals the Light,* a collection that includes the tale. To think of our origin merely as "something to break the monotony of his day," to imagine our most distant ancestors scared out of their wits, crammed in a clamshell (like rush-hour commuters in an LRT train), struck me as refreshingly, comically humbling.

Such humbling is of great value to the quintet of poets writing prose in *Thinking and Singing.* As I've re-read the book's vari-coloured mixture of pieces, that Haida tale –

as well as Reid's various art works based on it – has kept coming to mind. In one of his own essays printed here, Bringhurst writes: "Composing a poem is a way of leaving the self behind and getting involved in something larger." Both Bringhurst and Dennis Lee see polyphony – heard everywhere in natural and human cultures, and mimicked by poets – as one way to escape the cramping confines of singularity. To the editor of this book, Tim Lilburn, we need to practice "an activism of forgetting the royalty of one's name, of yielding, of stepping aside." In this book's predecessor, *Poetry and Knowing: Speculative Essays and Interviews,* also edited by Lilburn and including all the writers in this new book plus seven others, Jan Zwicky wrote: "Lyric thought and *humility* – Lyric celebrates the cosmos, not the perceiver thereof." One of the strongest desires in both books is to turn away from emphases on mind, imagination, art, and supreme fiction to the many debts we owe to – and the great responsibilities we should feel toward – "otherness" and "the cosmos." Those debts begin before infancy. Last week at the top of Sulphur Mountain outside Banff, after an air-gondola ride up the steep mountainside, my one-year-old daughter looked up when a Clark's nutcracker flew into view. Curiosity isn't the whole of it, but curiosity is a start.

The house in Calgary in which we're now vacationing has robins nesting in a lilac bush just outside the dining room window, and sharp-shinned hawks nesting near the cone-crowded top of a spruce tree across the street beyond the front yard. So I was amused and gladdened to find that Don McKay's essay, "The Bushtits' Nest," describes the nesting of a species he'd not encountered until recently. The interweaving of various bird nests seemed like a naïvely direct demonstration of what Bringhurst calls his own "very simpleminded belief that everything is related to everything else." In his essay, McKay, grounded by his helpful definition of ethics as "the calling-into-question of our freedom to control, process, or reduce the other," is less concerned with shirking off or sidestepping the self than with constructing respectful modes of interaction. His concession that "at bottom, a human perspective is impossible to escape" resembles Lee's speaking of not experiencing "a total whiteout of ego. The local *I* goes on." Still, McKay insists upon the need for "otherness kept scrupulously in mind." With the help of Levinas, he elaborates on *address* as an acknowledgment of limits to personal freedom, a nod to others' existence. "The other" is a key phrase not only for McKay but for all of this book, even in essays that don't explicitly employ it.

Meditating upon the intersections between poetry and philosophy, all five of the writers here chip away at human illusions of superiority. Lee expresses frustration with one recent example of such illusions, the assumption that "decentring monolithic systems is an achievement of postmodern thinkers and artists. Or that it's a human activity at all." Stories are "already decentred," argues Lee; "…being is plural, without or without our permission. Polyrhythm is no human creation. To think otherwise is hubris." There, the word is out: *hubris*. That word often lurks just beneath the surface of the prose in this book, such as when Jan Zwicky speaks in her first essay of Dao and Zen encouraging states of mind "free from the domination of ego," or when, more comically, in the mock-cowboy voice of the book's final piece, she puts question marks over pretensions that "Bein *needs* human language or it ain't gonna survive" or that "poets is more important in the scheme of things than small-eyed horny toads or cut-leaf sage." For years I've felt protest well up within me whenever I've re-read the section in "Nature" when Emerson says that it makes no difference whether "nature enjoy a substantial existence without, or is only an apocalypse of the mind." *But it does make a difference – a gigantic difference,* I've always felt like responding. So I clap and hoot assent from the back of the saloon when Zwicky's philosophical cowboy cuts down to size anyone who would claim status as "Author of the World."

¶ The other day, just before I began work on this introduction, a relative in the town of Linden, Alberta, gave me a photocopy from a column of doctor's advice, about how rock music damages children's hearing. Perhaps she thought it useful for my wife and me to read the report, though our children are still far from teenage years. But my eyes fell instead on another section of the good doctor's column, which referred to an article in *Smithsonian* magazine about an English stone-carver named Simon Verity who has talked of "listening to the stone" that he hammers and rubs away at. (Various pitches of sound signal qualities of the stone he's working on.) Like the Haida tale about the first men in a clamshell, the stone-carver's keen listening to stone (and how suggestive the name "Verity"!) quickly became a resonant backdrop to one reader's exploration of *Thinking and Singing.*

If the title of this book were to have a third verb, we might've ended up with *Thinking Listening Singing* – a tripartite title like Heidegger's "Building Dwelling Thinking." "Listening" is a word connected to "the other," since it's the other to whom we're encouraged to listen. ("The other," we might argue, is no more than an abstraction, since we're actually talking about countless *others.*) Listening may even provide the primary metaphor for receptivity to others' natures and histories, and thereby it's closely related to an escape from both egotism in the human realm and anthropocentrism in a broader context. In his preface, Lilburn notes that "a certain form of speech can be an attempt to hear" and that "Many poets say that poetry, too, is largely listening." Much later, he writes of the root cellar he made in the Moosewood Sandhills as "some sort of listening post," and of "a style that is so much ear, so attentive, it cannot step away from its listening and give a report of itself." Listening being more than merely a matter of the ears is evident in McKay's quotation from Chuang-tzu: "Rather than listening with the ear, listen with the heart. Rather than listening with the heart, listen with the energies." This takes synaesthesia a great distance. We listen not only to cries, calls, squeals, booms, and winnows in the air, but also to words on a page, memories, expectations, the unspoken desires and histories of other beings, and intimations not yet cut into language from whatever carvable stones we hold within us.

Rather than touting human consciousness and language(s) as the ultimate triumph of evolutionary progress, these poets find that the profoundest listenings are awake to the pre-linguistic. Lee believes that words start in a "pre-verbal flux," and that a poem "tries to enact that wordless tumble and surge [what Lee calls 'cadence'] in its own medium." All the writers here, it's easy to guess, would likely agree with Thoreau: "while we are confined to books, though the most select and classic, and read only particular languages, which are themselves but dialects and provincial, we are in danger of forgetting the language all things and events speak without metaphor, which alone is copious and standard." Even in our supposedly globalized age, all human languages, however widespread, are inherently provincial, since they're spoken only by our species (parrots and mynah birds aren't significant exceptions), and can only hint at the copious rhythms and interchanges of other species named and unnamed, as well as of everything formed from water, fire, air, and earth.

¶ Here and in their previous writings, the poets in this book have each tried to renovate or reroute certain familiar terms. We can cite Lee and "cadence," McKay and "wilderness," Lilburn and "eros," Zwicky and "lyric." Perhaps the most radical of the reroutings is Bringhurst's adaptation of the term "poetry" itself. Sometimes Bringhurst sees no distinction between poetry and genuine thinking: "Poetry *is* thinking, real thinking. And real thinking is poetry." At other times the denotations he gives to the term "poetry" are vaster yet. For Bringhurst in such passages, poetry is "not manmade ... not something hybridized by humans on the farm of human language. Poetry is a quality or aspect of existence." The things we call poems, Bringhurst concludes, "are the tips of the icebergs afloat on the ocean of poetry. But poetry continues to exist, maybe even to thrive, whether or not we deny or misdefine it." Perhaps Bringhurst's largest definitions of "poetry" are in fact deeply traditional, rooted in what Northrop Frye considered the most pervasive metaphor in Western culture: nature as book, scripture, riddle. We may find ourselves unable to embrace the magnitude of meaning Bringhurst applies to the term "poetry," but we need to grasp his use of it to appreciate the directions of his thought.

❡ The greatest satisfactions provided by *Thinking and Singing* include shocks of recognition and shocks of revelation. Readers may find themselves impressed or relieved or delighted to read particular passages. At times the poets here speak epigrammatically. I'll be grateful to remember Lee's "It's the all-at-oneness that gets you" and Bringhurst's "it is not the world's task to entertain us, but ours to take an interest in the world"; and I feel again like the raucous applauder at the back of Zwicky's saloon when McKay says: "We can, in short, try to be like Cézanne rather than Mount Rushmore." I'm also relieved to find Zwicky's acknowledgment, while wearing the cowboy-philosopher hat, that a leap of faith might be needed to escape the prison of mental configuring: "Yep, in the end no amount of analyzin's gonna tell you which way to jump…. You're picking a set of problems you'd rather live with: bein the front page story, or not being able to connect some kinds of knowin with logic. Seems to me thinkin we're the front page story ain't got such a hot track record." Ethics, much more than metaphysics, is essential to this book. In the end, Zwicky says, we take a "jump" in deciding whether we accept human intelligence as the key to the universe, or go instead for a humbler way, able to live with the shortcomings of logic and the perpetual incompleteness of our knowledge.

❡ In a 1951 piece on Wallace Stevens, Randall Jarrell wrote:

Poetry is a bad medium for philosophy. Everything in the philosophical poem has to satisfy irreconcilable requirements: for instance, the last demand that we should make of philosophy (that it be interesting) is the first we make of a poem; the philosophical poet has an elevated and methodical, but forlorn and absurd air as he works at his flying tank, his sewing-machine that also plays the piano.

Jarrell appears to make some troubling assumptions here – for instance, that a philosophical approach is always "elevated and methodical," and that philosophy shows no interest in being "interesting" (as if, for instance, Plato, Kant, Nietzsche, and Bergson wrote with utter indifference to their audience, with no awareness of using stylistic tools to provoke and hold their readers' attention). Also, despite the Dalí-esque whimsy in his imagery, the metaphor of philosophy as a sewing-machine may be more comic than Jarrell intended – comic at its own expense.

A century before Jarrell, Emerson also used a musical metaphor in dealing with intersections between poetry and philosophy, but his view was different:

The philosopher has a good deal of knowledge which cannot be abstractly imparted, which needs the combinations & complexity of social action to paint it out, as many emotions in the soul of Handel and Mozart are thousand voiced & utterly incapable of being told in a simple air on a lute ... so the philosopher avails himself of the drama, the epic, the novel, & becomes a poet; for these complex forms allow of the utterance of his knowledge of life by indirections *as well as in the didactic way, & can therefore express the fluxional quantities & values which the thesis or dissertation could never give.*

One of the more curious aspects of this passage from Emerson's journal is his comparing of a philosopher's prose to a lute's simple air; it's not the first metaphor most of us would adopt to describe the densities of, say,

Hegel or Wittgenstein. In finding greater capacities for polyphony, complexity, indirections, and "fluxional quantities" in the drama, the epic, the novel, than in more purely philosophical texts, Emerson is more positive about the possibility of philosophical poetry than Jarrell. Yet his metaphor is compromised by an assumption that philosophy is dominated by "thesis or dissertation," and by the oddity of the suggestion that it's single-voiced.

As a final, third use of a musical metaphor, let's employ a jazz musician much beloved by some of the writers in this book: philosophical poetry at its most attuned can be like Bill Evans's *Conversations with Myself,* in which Evans plays solo piano on top of a recording of his own solo piano. We hear two pianos together, not a sewing machine trying to be a piano.

It's clear than none of the poets in *Thinking and Singing* believe they're caught in a forlorn enterprise of "thinking vs. singing." For Lilburn, it's no strain to speak of "the eros which is philosophy," or of poetry as "the true way or a residual version of this [doing philosophy]." Bringhurst discusses other writers, such as Eliot and Vico, who thought the gulf between poetry and philosophy vast, and their simultaneity impossible. As a reply to Eliot, Vico, and Jarrell, we can quote Bringhurst: "In [Sophocles'] work, ideas dance and sing. That if anything ought to be what we mean by philosophical poetry." *Thinking and Singing* suggests that a hard-and-fast division between philosophy and poetry is one of those divisions – like those between poetry and prose, freedom and limitation, male and female, the conscious and the unconscious – that need ongoing qualification and questioning.

⁋ *Thinking and Singing* is a self-sufficient book, riveting in its own right, kaleidoscopic in its approaches. But it's also the continuation of a conversation present in the earlier compilation, *Poetry and Knowing*. Readers who haven't read the earlier book would do well to do so after – or before – reading this one; readers who have completed both, in order, would then do well to re-read the first. Many sentences from the 1995 book can illuminate passages in the new one. We should remember McKay's "It is as dangerous to act as though we were not a part of nature as it is to act as if we were not a part of culture"; equally quotable is Zwicky's "Philosophy without passion is bookkeeping in the history of ideas." As a gloss on Bringhurst's discussion here of the poetry/philosophy mix, there's this from Zwicky's contribution to the earlier book: "Within the domain of lyrically expressed thought, the distinction between poetry and philosophy has no meaning." Bringhurst himself supplied an earlier passage to stand alongside passages in the new book that emphasize both humility and listening: "Knowing freed from the agenda of possession and control – knowing in the sense of stepping in tune with being, hearing and echoing the music and heartbeat of being – is what we mean by poetry." Note that this definition differs from those of Bringhurst outlined earlier. For Bringhurst, clearly, "poetry" is a term that sometimes changes its stripes or, like some mythical beast, undergoes metamorphoses.

⁋ Another morning. The nests are now empty, and robins are calling sharply from the back yard, hawks crying *kik-kik-kik-kik-kik-kik* from the front yard. In the house where those bird voices meet, I'm listening again to the thinking and singing of five poets, who've listened to each other while listening to whatever floats in, literally audible or inaudible, through the windows of their houses. All over the place, things are being said with or without words. Listen. One of countless places to start is with the welcome voices in this book.

SOURCES

Section VI of Emerson's "Nature" and the chapter "Sounds" in Thoreau's *Walden,* both available in many editions. Also, *Emerson in His Journals,* ed. Joel Porte (Cambridge, MA: Harvard University Press, 1982): p 217; Randall Jarrell, "Reflections on Wallace Stevens," in *Wallace Stevens: The Critical Heritage,* ed. Charles Doyle (London: Routledge and Kegan Paul, 1985): pp 333–4; Bill Reid and Robert Bringhurst, *The Raven Steals the Light* (Vancouver: Douglas & McIntyre, 2nd ed., 1996): p 34.

I

Dennis Lee

Body Music:
Notes on Rhythm in Poetry

I · KINAESTHETIC KNOWING

1

What makes a poem cohere? How does it mean what it means?

It starts where the poem does: in the preverbal flex and coherence the words arise from. A poem tries to enact that wordless tumble and surge in its own medium – in line breaks and pauses, syntax and sound, the ripple and clarion strut of sense on the page. It tries to recreate the cadence of how things are, through the nitty-gritty of craft.

But how do you get a handle on that? How can you understand technique as more than just a bag of tricks? As witness, and cosmology, and desire?

2

It starts with rhythm, that much I know. I mean the way the poem moves in time – its pace and gait and proportions. A poem can unfold with the shapely aplomb of a gavotte, or meander, or move with a quicksilver stutter and glide. Each rhythm shapes the energy flow with a distinct logic; each parses the world with a syntax of its own. A poem thinks by the way it moves.

But that raises another question, for rhythmic logic is not conceptual. How can you translate its native terms into categories your mind can deal with? How do you talk about moves your body grasps in a flash?

3

I'm drawn to terms like these.

Prosody as sonic improvisation. Polyrhythmic form. A kinetics of meaning: clenched, a galumph, then wash of a liminal segue. Forward momentum; lateral gusts. Kinaesthetic knowing. Trajectories in audio space. Scoring the energy spoor. The rhythmic manifold. A poetics of voice in motion. Cosmophony. Body music.

4

Acts of rhythmic attention comprise a syntax for knowing the world.

5

How do we apprehend rhythm?

It's customary to take the auditory sense as primary. We "hear the beat," we say – and so we do. But that's too restricted. We need to include the rhythmic experience of the whole body. This involves hearing, and sometimes sight and touch. But more fundamentally, it involves the way our muscles register pressure, torsion, stress, pulsation, movement; the way they distinguish a throb from a lurch from a zoom.

We experience texture and periodicity right at the muscular level – with our kinaesthetic sense. Our body becomes the instrument the rhythm is played on; we register it viscerally, absorb it as carnal knowledge.

*

And we know a certain inner experience, which unfolds with no external stimulus to the organ involved. Thus we "hear with our inner ear," we "see with the third eye." Most of us could listen to a favourite song right now inside our heads, and talk about the experience. This faculty is vital when it comes to poetry – and nowhere more than with the muscular sense. We can experience a tumble and carom and surge without physical prompting, as I can attest. Yet the faculty has no name, informal or technical.

What to call this intuitive kinaesthetic sense – *kinesense? body music? kintuition?* I don't have the right term yet, but the faculty is normative.

6

How we scan the world.

How a poem's music makes a statement of its own – before, beneath, and shot-through the particular content. A second language.

It says: the world comes in chunks. Or *glissando*. Or, there is a deep current. Or a hush. Or cacophony. It says …

7

Prosody rhymes with cosmology. I know that's so, but I can't yet say what it means.

8

I remember poring over Pound and Williams in the early sixties. The way their poems moved – what the hell were they *doing*? I found their rhythms foreign, since my ear had been shaped by traditional poetry. Yet I knew I had to connect. I was trying to write, but my hunches didn't jibe with the older rhythmic language.

By the time I caught up with my immediate elders, Purdy and Creeley & Co., I'd begun to acclimatize to the modern soundscape. Mind you, most poets of my generation had been attuned to it for years. But I didn't feel an automatic rapport with their body music. And when I did, it was scary. I opened John Newlove's *Moving in Alone* in 1965, and I wanted to kneecap the man. Assassinate him. Here was a poet my own age, with moves so cleanly etched I could feel them probing the reflexes of my work, exposing its mannered stiffness. How had he learned to write like that?

Since then I've found my way to a kinaesthetic language that feels more like home. But when I test the poetic rhythms of the last hundred years – body-scan them, so to speak – I still get mixed signals. There are modes that feel continuous with the way things are. There are others that feel alien. And there are rhythms I know firsthand that don't show up in the accepted accounts at all.

That's part of what I want to reckon with now: this inside/outside relation to the norms of modern rhythm.

9

There is a craft of scoring energy on the page. You orchestrate the flow; you coax it to enact the dance.

10

The poetry I mean to explore exists first of all on the page; its native medium is print.

One thing is so obvious, it's seldom discussed. That is, while page poetry is a temporal medium, its sequence unfolds in space as well as time. A poem's specific rhythms emerge when you start at line one, read from left to right, and make your way down the page to the end. The poem unfolds in time, but its unfolding is enacted in space; the two dimensions are interdependent.

But the ratio of interdependence is not a constant. In classical English poetry, the spatial dimension seldom claims our attention. In modern poetry, by contrast, temporal and spatial aspects are conspicuously fused. The rhythms of a modern poem could not exist outside its spatial dimension.

But I'm jumping ahead. For now, it's enough to observe that poetic rhythm unfolds in spatio-temporal terms.

11

The order you sense in cadence is more like a passage of music, or a movement of dance, than a geometrical figure.

What the poem mimes is not a static structure, but an active cohering. Kinetic rhythms of being. A cosmophony, more than a cosmology.

12

In the mid-nineteenth century, a few poets began to chafe at the grammar of rhythmic coherence which had obtained for hundreds of years. Working in isolation, the best found alternative rhythms. And in the first two decades of the twentieth, the process reached a crescendo, creating a new rhythmic logic for poetry. This paralleled developments in other fields – physics, music, painting – where the basic grammar of coherence was likewise being transformed. "Modern poetry" means poetry which participates in this transformation of rhythmic norms.

The transformation was achieved in the composition of particular poems. Critical analysis is still catching up.

*

- *Classical English poetry.* Poetry written in traditional rhythmic syntax. Classical poetry extends, with many permutations, from Chaucer to the present.

- *Modern English poetry.* Poetry that works with a range of non-classical rhythmic intuitions. It extends from at least Whitman to the present; thus it overlaps in time with recent classical poetry. And many poets now use rhythmic conventions from both traditions. (The usage is different from "modern thought," which refers to the form and content of thinking since about 1600.)

- *Modernist poetry.* The first fully developed generation of modern poetry – Pound, Eliot, Williams, etc. The high period was roughly 1915–1950. Because of a particular technical advance, which we'll come to soon, we can say that the modernists initiated modern poetry proper.

13

You steer by your ear. By your kinaesthetic ear.

There are actual rhythms, in known poems, that are world-instigating. But some don't appear on the orthodox maps of the rhythmic continuum. What's more, there are modern rhythms that have yet to be enacted.

We have only begun to explore this new acoustic space.

14

Rich rhythmic manifold: how to score the plenum? The frequencies of being?

The dance of simultaneous wavelengths – how to honour them at once?

15

In a poem of any length, different kinds of rhythm unfold simultaneously. They operate at different scales, each with its own language. As a working distinction:

- *Micro-rhythms*: the fine-scale rhythms that organize syllables, words, a line, several lines.

- *Mezzo-rhythms*: the rhythms that obtain on a middle scale – from several lines to half a page. (As an example, the rhythms of a stanza or a verse paragraph.)

- *Macro-rhythms*: the rhythms that orchestrate parts within the whole.

*

I want to explore the rhythmic syntax of poetry at each of these scales; and specifically, to track the change of syntax from classical to modern.

II · MICRO-RHYTHM: PROSODY

16

It starts with *prosody*. The fundamental rhythmic syntax.

There are dictionary definitions, all of them based on classical practice. But for our present purposes, they're too narrow. What I mean by prosody is *the craft of orchestrating micro-rhythms*.

*

Why start with prosody?

Because it's the basis for everything else. The deep matrix. You can't write a two-page poem without a feel for macro-rhythms. But without a feel for micro-rhythms, you can't write two lines. The poem's shoelaces are tied together; six words on a page just sit there – or they clunk along, an arbitrary sequence of syllables.

*

In classical English poetry, micro-rhythms were organized by metrical prosody. In modern poetry, they're organized on a different basis.

Arriving at a new prosody was the basic technical step in the invention of modern poetry, the most profoundly enabling. And it was part of a general shift in our intuition of coherence.

That larger shift intrigues me, though I'll concentrate here on its manifestation in poetry: the change from classical prosody to modern.

17

To fathom metrical prosody, you can't just rehearse the scansion of specific feet and meters, like we did in grade ten. Nor simply retrace the history of its development since 1400, compelling though that is. You have to explore how poets were *using* this rhythmic language: how it let them scan the world. And what they heard.

18

The basis of metrical prosody was a particular element of rhythm: the stress or intensity with which we pronounce individual syllables. Traditionally, two degrees of intensity were recognized – strong and weak. The micro-rhythm of classical English poetry was based on the organization of strong and weak syllabic stresses.

But you have to go further than that. As I understand it, metrical prosody was a craft of improvisation, in which two different systems of syllabic stress were syncopated against each other. Two "protocols," I'll call them (since one was not a system at all). One protocol was fixed, the other variable.

- The fixed protocol was the meter, or "measure." It gave an abstract model for the rhythm of each line – a pre-established sequence of strong and weak beats. Iambic pentameter, trochaic tetrameter, whatever.

Each meter consisted of *x*-many feet, or syllabic units. And since it repeated the same foot throughout, the metrical rhythm was completely regular.

A reader recognized this underlying measure in the first few lines – kinaesthetically, not analytically. Its beat went on ticking in the reader's body sense for the rest of the poem, like a ghostly metronome. (In iambic pentameter: *da*-DUM / *da*-DUM / *da*-DUM / *da*-DUM / *da*-DUM.) And this furnished the ground bass for whatever syllabic rhythms actually ensued. The distinction is important, since no poet reproduced the metrical pattern beat for beat, unless he was very naïve.

- The second, variable protocol consisted of the stresses found in the actual words of the poem – pronounced as they are in ordinary speech. This protocol was unprogrammed, and irregular. Some of its stresses coincided with those of the metrical pattern (weak or strong); others diverged from it. But providing they didn't deviate for too long, the reader continued to sense the meter ticking.

- What metrical poets developed was a craft of *syncopation*: of counterpointing the flux of spoken stresses against the regular metrical beat, so they kept dancing in and out of phase in the reader's body-sense. This syncopation unfolded largely beneath his threshold of conscious attention – keeping the subliminal microrhythms carnal and vivacious. The more resourceful the poet, the more compelling the dance.

19

The sophistication and richness of metrical craft take my breath away. Even though it's not my native language, except in children's poetry.

20

The natural unit of meter was the line. So you can observe the prosody at work by auditing a single line:

Let me not to the marriage of true minds ...

You pick up the syncopation most readily if you try inflecting the line by the iambic pattern alone, and observe the nonsensical singsong that results:

Let ME / *not* TO / *the* MAR- / (*ri*)*age* OF / *true* MINDS ...

That's grotesque. But nobody reads the line that way. And when you speak it more naturally – however you inflect it exactly; there's no single right way, which means the reader too must improvise – the spoken stresses and the metrical beat move in and out of phase. The strong accent may shift to a different position within a foot. Three syllables will skip along in the metrical space reserved for two. There may be no strong spoken stress at all in a syllabic group where the meter makes us hear one. There are speed-ups and hesitations. The syncopated microrhythms emerge as shifting and alive.

*

What determines the moment-to-moment syncopation?

At one level, it's simply the standard pronunciation of words – which coincides with the metrical beat for a foot or two, then sets up a counter-rhythm, then returns to the meter. But since nothing obliged the poet to use precisely these words, the explanation is correct but beside the point.

Finally, all you can say is that some deep, spontaneous delight in improvisation configures the micro-rhythms. Kintuition, I'll call it. Kinaesthetic play.

21

What sense of coherence is manifest here?

It's possible to discern signature moves in the prosody of individual poets, and these enact the syntax of order that each intuits. But going further: how is coherence parsed in metrical prosody at large? What underlying scansion of the world does it embody?

It says, there is a fixed order. And at the same time, there is a flux: of freedom, of chaos, of both. Truth in rhythm consists of orchestrating order and flux at once.

Two rhythmic protocols: one fixed, one variable. Without meter, measure, degree – without some residual sense of natural law, holding the world together – the freeplay of particulars would degenerate into chaos. Without unscheduled play, structure would become an iron grid. It is within this kintuition, of established order and freedom entwined, that rhythmic meaning emerges in metrical poetry.

For centuries, this cosmophony governed the micro-rhythm of poetry. And in broad terms, it seems to me, it meshed with the sense of the world's coherence which persisted in Europe during its ascendancy: the sense that things were free to be themselves within the natural law established by God.

22

That was one kintuition of coherence. But the centre ceased to hold; in the body sense of more and more poets, the world no longer moved that way. And that intrigues me. What were they picking up? How did they know what they knew?

Whatever the explanation, a crisis in rhythmic norms ensued. After 1850, some poets began to grope for a different syntax of micro-rhythms. This produced a flurry of unrelated experiments in prosody, some of them non-metrical. But sixty years later, even the best remained isolated achievements. They were like beautiful, sideways evolutionary mutations – each of which established a niche of its own, but none of which became the primary line of development.

*

The most important innovations were Whitman's dithyrambic line, and Hopkins's sprung verse. But Hopkins was unrepeatable. And while Whitman's line tantalized later poets, it swamped almost everyone who tried it; only Lawrence, Jeffers, Ginsberg would find their own way.

Other new prosodies were arbitrary, like the non-metrical syllabics which Marianne Moore devised. And there was a scatter of backward-looking experiments. Some poets tried to modify the status quo by exhuming

Latin meter. And around 1910, Eliot developed his own subtle modification of metrical prosody.

All these mutations bubbled up in the shift from classical to modern micro-rhythm. In the case of Whitman, Hopkins, Eliot, the new prosodies engendered great poetry, but mainly by their creators. None of them furnished a rhythmic language which poets of widely varied persuasions could use. And the other innovations were sports, or tours de force, rather than live new rhythmic languages.

*

If we freeze the frame in 1910, we get this picture. It was still possible for poets of the first rank to work in meter – as Yeats was doing, and Stevens later would. But for the growing number of poets who had lost access to that language, there was no prosody that let them move naturally on the page.

23

Losing pentameter wasn't the problem. The problem was, losing iambic. With the metronome gone, the syllable came unmoored.

24

It's not surprising that some poets tried to cope by tinkering with traditional prosody. To give up meter altogether, without some potent alternative galvanizing you – that brought on vertigo. There was nothing to steer by. Consider:

- Without that steady underbeat as the norm, what governs the rhythm of syllables? Is there any music left that's specific to poetry? Aren't you just writing prose, chopped into shorter and longer lines?

- What is a line of verse, when there's no fixed measure? How do you know where to end one string of words and start the next? If you can break a line after the tenth word, why not after the eighth? or the second? Why not divide it into ten itty-bitty lines, each of a single word?

- The more deeply you enter post-metrical listening, the blurrier things get. The left-hand margin, for instance: what anchors it now? If you're no longer heading back to that fixed point to start a new metrical run, what necessity does it have? Why should a line start at the far left? Why should it start in *any* specific position? But if it's cut adrift, where does it come to rest? The whole prosodic logic of the poem has become impossibly fluid. The white space of the page starts to feel like a deeper-breathing silence, with this aimless welter of words slipsliding around in it.

Without meter, what is the basis of rhythmic coherence – *any* basis? *any* coherence? How should syllables move on the page? Put differently: how does the world cohere? What are the categories in which it makes sense? Or are there any?

25

The breakthrough came with the discovery of free verse.

The term has a varied history. But I take it to mean poetry written in a new prosody, which Ezra Pound developed between 1912 and 1920 (following French examples, and experiments by Hilda Doolittle). The system spread like gossip, becoming the non-metrical prosody of choice in the English-speaking world. It embodied a new kintuition of order.

26

I call this new system *scoring*, or *free prosody*. Poets have been using it for almost a century now. But deciphering how it works is still a challenge.

If I've got it straight, scoring proceeds by syncopating two rhythmic protocols, as metrical prosody did. But there the resemblance ends. You can't understand scoring by looking for equivalents to metrical categories; it's an entirely different way of hearing micro-rhythm.

*

In broad terms, its features are these:

- One rhythmic protocol draws on patterns of speech; the other depends on line breaks and layout on the page. These can be termed syntax and notation respectively.

- Both protocols are variable. That is, the prosody is free.

- The focus is not on syllabic stress, but on "pointing." On the rhythms of local attention. When the two protocols are syncopated, the pointing of one is played against the pointing of the other.

- The natural unit of scoring is not the line, but a sequence of two or more lines.

In this vocabulary: scoring improvises the pointing of micro-rhythms, through the interplay of syntax and notation.

27

A director "points" the flow of a scene on the stage. A violinist points a passage of a sonata. They etch the rhythms cleanly, bring out specific textures and dynamics. Otherwise the performance is muddy, lumpy, lacks focus.

Pointing controls for two things: pacing and emphasis. Pacing includes speed – slower or faster; momentum – the force of advance; tempo – the cumulative changes in speed and momentum. And emphasis includes the darts or swirls of attention which guide us to focus on *this* word, *this* moment, *this* pool of feeling, and to glide past others.

When a passage is pointed well, it's impossible to say where pacing ends and emphasis begins. They're different names for the same dynamics.

*

Mind you, a live performance has resources for pointing which don't exist on the page. Volume and timbre and pitch; physical movement; body language. A page poem would kill for them, but it can't have them. It has other things instead.

28

What do the protocols of pointing in free prosody consist of?

We know what we mean by syntax: the arrangement of grammatical parts in a sentence. The way subject and verb and object organize what's being expressed; the way phrases and clauses are massed and counterweighted. The syntax points the meaning with a specific kinetic logic.

And I'll expand the term, to include the way consecutive sentences are marshalled. That creates a further range of syntactic pointing. Two quick sentences, leading to a mighty periodic surge. Staccato question: staccato reply. If the words are savvy, their syntax guides us through a specific rhythm of attention.

*

But what determines the syntax of a free poem?

That's like asking what governs the spoken stresses in a metrical poem. In a sense, both are generated by the content. But that's just the point of departure. The poet is goosed along by an intuitive *something* – in scoring, to jump ahead, by the rhythmic dance that's itching to happen, if he can get the syntax talking to the notation the way they're straining to.

What generates the syntax is the open-ended tug and *telos* of improvisation. No recipes; no nets.

Finally, it is governed by the poet's kintuition of cadence. By the tumble and play of what is. The body music of world.

29

What about the pointing created by notation?

As we saw above, in post-metrical poetry you can point the words in a dizzying variety of ways, depending on how you set them up on the page. The pacing and emphasis change as you vary the spatial layout, sometimes dramatically, sometimes almost imperceptibly. Yet the actual elements of notation are few in number.

- The basic element is the line break. Its placement determines the length of the line. It also affects the pace: speeding it up, slowing it down, shifting it from measured to headlong. And it affects the emphasis, particularly if the break comes in the middle of a unit of sense; a slightly heightened stress falls on the first word of the next line. Many free-verse poets notate exclusively with line breaks.

- If they go further, the next element is the margin: which lines to indent; how far. This sets up an additional level of pointing, creating parallel or off-centre relationships among the lines. And it affects the pace, because it governs the return time: how long it takes the eye to swing back to the beginning of the next line.

- Two other elements appear less frequently: internal spaces within a line, and deployment of the white space of the page as an active component, connoting silence.

30

To hear free prosody at work, you have to listen to several lines. Here's Pound in the *Pisan Cantos*, scoring open notation against the syntax:

> *... and the news is a long time moving*
>   *a long time in arriving*
>   *thru the impenetrable*
> *crystalline, indestructible*
>   *ignorance of locality*
> *The news was quicker in Troy's time*
> *a match on Cnidos, a glow worm on Mitylene....*

The syntax points the sense with a deliberate, measured movement, as the three sets of parallel phrases unfold. And at the same time, the line breaks and staggered margins point the sense with a second logic – which sometimes meshes with the syntax, sometimes plays across it. The two protocols marry on the page, creating a flow of rhythmic attention which is almost liturgical, yet locally alive.

No other poem will repeat this particular scoring; each move in free prosody is a one-shot improvisation. But the language of syntax-and-notation is wonderfully flexible. It's hard to do well, but it allows a poet room to orchestrate micro-rhythms in the key of whatever. It gives poets of many different persuasions a language to work in.

31

This account of scoring leaves several loose ends to sort out.

When you read a free poem out loud, it's often difficult to translate the spatial notation into physical sound. Line breaks are dicey; indents are impossible. As a result, much of the pointing gets flattened out in a live reading. It is fully accessible only in the original, spatio-temporal medium, where the notation can be seen.

At the same time, there are new resources when you read aloud, such as volume and pitch. A free poem is aural, but on the page it can only gesture at some of its own vocal shading.

This means that to experience a free poem in its home medium, you have to *hear it out loud on the page*. You have to absorb its movement with the eye, the inner ear, and the body sense at once.

32

In the passage from Pound, the last line was in iambic pentameter: "a match on Cnidos, a glow worm on Mitylene." We sense the five-beat pattern behind the words; each reader will syncopate the spoken stresses against that abstract measure in his own way.

But if the poem is in free verse, how can this be?

There's no law against shifting into meter in free verse. Some poets never do; others do for a phrase, a line, even a short passage. But when this happens, how should we specify the prosody? I understand it thus:

- The poem's entire movement is governed by free prosody. It is scored throughout.

- When it passes through a metrical patch, it's both scored and metrical. Within that local domain, it obeys both prosodies at once.

- In a comparable way, the laws of Newtonian space obtain locally within Einsteinian space-time.

33

In free verse, syllables are stressed as they are in metrical poetry – by their spoken pronunciation. This brings something else to light.

There are only so many patterns that syllabic stresses can fall into; hence you still find dactyls and spondees and iambs in free verse. But these are not metrical feet. They are something we don't have a name for yet: units of spoken stress.

These patterns of emphasis can be artfully deployed in a poem, but that doesn't mean they're being syncopated against a background meter. The whole telephone book can be analyzed into spoken iambs and trochees and anapests; it's still not a metrical composition. It is only when a line is unmistakably syncopated against a known meter – "a match on Cnidos, a glow worm on Mitylene" – that it is metrical.

34

This brings us to the primary question: how is coherence parsed in free prosody? Beyond the signature moves of individual poets, what scansion of the world does it enact?

What's new in free prosody is that there is no fixed measure. Both protocols are variable. And while each can become regular for a spell, that is simply one possibility within the rhythmic continuum. It doesn't define the continuum per se.

Free prosody says, the world is coherent – but its coherence emerges in the interplay of variable systems of order. There is no absolute measure which antedates the poem. Coherence is local, provisional, contingent in the flux.

This is a new kintuition of order: polyvalent and relative. It gives the distinctive cosmophony of modern rhythm. And in ways I can glimpse, if only dimly, it meshes with the account of the world's coherence which has emerged in the last century. It resonates with the formal intuitions of relativity and quantum mechanics, where an absolute frame of reference no longer exists.

III · MEZZO-RHYTHM: FORWARD/LATERAL ACTION

35

It's time to sharpen some distinctions:

- *Kinaesthesia*: the sensation in the muscles produced by direct physical pressure, movement, pulsation.

- *Body music*: the inner experience of kinaesthetic rhythm, when there is no literal stimulus to the muscles. The occasion may be reading a poem, or listening to music. Or it can be triggered by memory or kintuition.

- *Kintuition*: kinaesthetic intuition. The capacity to register rhythm with no identifiable mediation, direct or indirect. This might sound like mystification, if it weren't the normal working experience of many artists.

*

I also use "body music" in two extended senses:

- The kinaesthetic dimension of a poem.
- The rhythmic coherence of what is. The body music of world. Cadence; cosmophony. It is to this, I believe, that kintuition responds.

36

Rich rhythmic manifold: how to score the plenum?
    Acts of rhythmic attention are a species of natural prayer. Cosmophony and desire.

37

The modernist innovators discovered a brave new rhythmic world. But it was not exhaustively defined by the poems they wrote, nor the theories they devised.
    What's more, our current map of the modern tradition – which shows it originating with Whitman, coming into its own in Pound, Eliot, and Williams, and then fanning out through the ramifications of the new American poetry – is not a trustworthy guide. Or not, at least, when it comes to modern rhythm at the mezzo- and macro-scales. That account identifies achievements which are there, and deserve to be celebrated. But it closes off the continuum of rhythmic possibilities to a claustrophobic degree.

38

Radio space. The air alive with waves, vibrations.

So too there are frequencies of being.

Step 1: a way of moving that can tune to this plural energy, and let it shape the movement of the poem. Enacting first one frequency, then another, then the next.

Step 1002: what makes you crazy – how to write the world as it *is*. Not consecutive, but overlaid. How cadence teems on simultaneous wavelengths: slalom and moloch and crouch. *And* torque. *And* soar....

The challenge is, how to enact a polyrhythmic body music?

39

It's the all-at-onceness that gets you. When you're attuned, the many-plied rhythms issue an impossible directive: utter us utterly. Dance all of us – now, in words, at once.

It is in light of that kintuition that a poem of any length works for me or doesn't. Before I attend to anything else, I crave a music that inhabits polyrhythm as a denizen.

But how to honour that directive on the page?

40

I want now to jostle our map of sonic space, to make a particular mezzo-rhythm audible.

Anyone who has been claimed by the moves I speak of will know why they matter. They coexist with the micro-rhythms of prosody. But they organize the trajectory of the poem on a larger scale, in passages of ten or twenty lines. And they employ an entirely different rhythmic language.

41

The mezzo-rhythm I have in mind is what I call *compound rhythm*. Or *composite movement*. Or *forward/lateral action*.

In broad terms, it occurs when one energy propels the poem down the page – and gets simultaneously buffeted, transected, deformed by a series of lateral gusts. These cross-energies multiply the flow, and redirect the original momentum. The effect is to make us experience two or more energies at once: to make the poem polyrhythmic. We start to hear what could be called "rhythmic harmonics."

*

Take a relatively straightforward example, still in general terms. Suppose one train of thought is underway. And suppose it is invaded – conceptually and syntactically – by a second train of thought, which comes in from a different angle. The poem assimilates this incursion, and continues its (altered) course. As it does, we feel the new thought powering the advance at the same time as the original. Both energies, forward and lateral, now propel the poem; its rhythm is compound.

And the energies don't have to be conceptual. There may be a tidal wave of feeling – of celebration, perhaps – which surges ahead in cresting rhythms. Yet a series of nagging underfeelings begin to declare themselves, cutting across the ongoing flow with dissident moves and tonalities.

Or the poem proceeds by a series of minute discriminations – but then gets blindsided by a larger prophetic afflatus. Or a blurt of grief. Or whatever. Both modes of locomotion continue as the poem proceeds.

These lateral dynamics can be of any kind: shifts of voice; sudden memories; associative musings, touched off by something as slight as a double take on the sound of a word. They are heterogeneous in nature. And the crosshatched energies begin to mime the plenum, the polyphasic cadence of what is.

42

Who has written this way? This amounts to asking, what would a truer map of rhythmic ancestors look like? When I scan the continuum with that in mind, it leads me outside English poetry.

As far as I can tell, the first modern master of compound mezzo-rhythm was Friedrich Hölderlin. Starting in the late 1790s, his freefall through a new cadential space was enacted so potently on the page, I can give pride of ancestral place to no one but him. The stricken tremendum he tracked in his elegies and odes is kinaesthetically richer than much of what has happened since. Our map of usable ancestors should be expanded to recognize his polyrhythmic innovations.

*

No short excerpt can do justice to Hölderlin's body music. But here is one stanza from "Patmos." He is speaking of the death of Christ, and the subsequent withdrawal of the sacred from the daily world. Beyond the content, however, the rhythm tells a story of its own. A torrential energy hurtles down the page; at the same time, cross-energies swarm – splaying the syntax, and dissolving normal connectives:

> *Wenn aber stirbt alsdenn*
> *An dem am meisten*
> *Die Schönheit hing, daß an der Gestalt*
> *Ein Wunder war und die Himmlischen gedeutet*
> *Auf ihn, und wenn, ein Räthsel ewig füreinander,*
> *Sie sich nicht fassen können*
> *Einander, die zusammenlebten*
> *Im Gedächtniß, und nicht den Sand nur oder*
> *Die Weiden es hinwegnimmt und die Tempel*
> *Ergreifft, wenn die Ehre*
> *Des Halbgotts und der Seinen*
> *Verweht und selber sein Angesicht*
> *Der Höchste wendet*
> *Darob, daß nirgend ein*
> *Unsterbliches mehr am Himmel zu sehn ist oder*
> *Auf grüner Erde, was ist diß?*

Christopher Middleton catches much of the parasyntactic whirl and crossfire of the original:

> *But when he dies then*
> *To whom beauty*
>   *Most clung, making his form*
> *Flesh of a miracle*
>   *And the powers of heaven*
> *Pointed to him, and when, eternally*
>   *Riddles to one another, they*
>   *Cannot grasp one another, who*
> *Lived as one*

> *In memory, and when it takes away*
> *Not the sand only, nor the willows,*
> *When it takes hold*
> *Of the temples, when the demigod*
> *And his own are all*
> *Stript of honor, and even the Highest*
> *Averts his gaze, whence not a shred*
> *Of immortality is seen in heaven or on*
> *The green earth, what is this?*

Even Middleton's admirable version domesticates Hölderlin's torrent: tames the tumble of clauses with added punctuation, corrals the lunge and yaw of the syntax more quickly than does the original. Still, the forward/lateral action is unmistakable.

*

As the German demonstrates, Hölderlin appears to have arrived at free scoring a hundred years before Pound. But we'll set questions of micro-rhythm aside, and focus on what's taking place at the mezzo-scale. Across the whole stanza, the syntax bucks and swivels. The poem moves in a welter of simultaneous energies.

What are these energies?

One answer would be: the ideas Hölderlin is expressing. Because they are complex, the syntax has to be complex to articulate them. But that's not good enough. For a start, the passage doesn't "express ideas." It presents events in the sacred history of the West, in a densely visionary mode. And more than that: if Hölderlin was simply trying to communicate this content, there's no reason he couldn't have organized it more straightforwardly. A copy editor could easily improve the stanza – breaking it into three or four shorter sentences, supplying connectives, and resolving these syntactic air-pockets where we seem to hang in space, propelled in two or three directions at once.

Needless to say, the improvements would gut the poem. Hölderlin himself was taken aback by the music he found himself obeying. But as he declared (in a headnote to "Friedensfeier"), "If some should think such speech too unconventional, I must confess to them: I cannot help it." That is: whatever these energies may consist of, their whiplash dynamics possess a life of their own. Hölderlin's task was to let them play through the poem as cleanly as possible. For at the deepest level, their compound music *was* the poem – sustaining and animating everything else.

This stands as pure kintuition: direct apprehension of a body music that lies beneath or beyond the actual words, and furnishes the rhythms by which they move. If it were not for the composite movement of the poem, we might never know these energies existed. But there they palpably are, commingling in its trajectory.

Calling them "energies" is merely a way of saluting their cosmophonic source. I wish I had a better term to pay it homage. But in any case, this way of moving taps into a rich and plural sonic space – one whose polyrhythms are enacted directly on the page.

43

What kintuition does compound rhythm bespeak?

It says, there is always *more*. The frequencies of being

are a sounding plethora. No matter how mobile the poetic line, the energies that attune it are more multiform, more simultaneous than consciousness can hope to organize. Reality is richer than all of our formulations of reality. And compound rhythm declares this, not by asserting it conceptually, but by enacting it kinaesthetically. In the dangerous rhythms of more.

This is voice with its life on the line. Shipwrecked ekstasis: manifold being, at once.

44

The source of poetic authority here is not Friedrich Hölderlin. It is the polyrhythmic cadence of what is.

So it is not that everyone else should try to sound like Hölderlin. God spare us another orthodoxy, one more sure-fire technique. The point is that the kinaesthetic space he skidded into, two hundred years ago, is far richer than our current maps recognize. The truest response is not to imitate him, but to attend to the polyrhythmic energy of what is. Given such attending, many different musics can emerge within the syntax of compound rhythm.

To write like Hölderlin today would mean accepting the directive: utter us utterly. With no blueprint for what the poem should sound like.

45

And I got drunk on that sonic niagara. From my twenties on, Hölderlin and Pindar (in translation; my Greek is too spotty) were my rhythmic *Lear*.

46

Some features of compound rhythm emerge more clearly if we set it beside free prosody, comparing them as modern grammars of coherence on different scales.

- Scoring syncopates two protocols, both variable; compound rhythm orchestrates unprogrammed energies. That is, neither relies on a fixed measure to calibrate the rhythm.

- That said, there appears to be nothing in composite rhythm corresponding to the twin protocols of syntax and notation. Its energies are all over the map. At the mezzo-scale, the counterpoint of forward/lateral action does not unfold within a binary framework.

- The specifically modern innovation in prosody was the shift from fixed/variable to variable/variable. Has there been a comparable change in compound rhythm? You can find forward/lateral movement in classical verse; think of *Paradise Lost*. But has its nature changed in modern practice? Or is the difference chiefly that compound rhythm now draws on free prosody, rather than meter?

    I don't have clarity on this question. But as a poet, I'm not particularly concerned to figure it out. What takes precedence is the sheer fact of polyrhythm, which issues its luminous perpetual directive.

- Both scoring and compound rhythm give poets room to improvise in whatever key they're drawn to. That is, neither is tied to a single audition of coherence. Each furnishes a syntax for many kinds of body music; each lets us score the rhythmic harmonics in a multitude of ways.

And in fact, forward/lateral action has been practised in varying forms by a wide range of modern poets – none of whom sounds like Hölderlin, or like the others. I think of poets as different as William Carlos Williams, Robert Creeley, Al Purdy, Ed Dorn, Gerald Stern, Don McKay, to name just a handful. It would be a treat to trace the varieties of compound rhythm in their work, though it would take more space than I can devote to it here.

47

So it is not that we lack precedents for modern mezzo-polyrhythm. But our poetics ignore the precedents that are already there. Our map of the modern continuum leaves crucial rhythms inaudible; it screens out the primacy of body music by ignoring so much of its basic language.

We've got to ventilate this place.

48

In Hölderlin's poetry, it's the structure of the sentence that is constantly getting recast. His compound rhythms exert their pressure chiefly on the syntax; other dimensions of the poem are much less affected. We could compare him to a jazz soloist who improvises on the melody, but keeps to the original time signature, and plays with a uniform timbre.

That's one way of doing forward/lateral action, and it has the authority of origin. But the clash and convergence of energies can unfold in other dimensions as well.

49

One such dimension is *voice*. The energies that enter the poem can splay the syntax; they can also roughen or pucker or deepen the tonality. The poem will then register their presence as a series of shifting phonic disturbances. And the trajectory of the poem will be naturally polyphonic.

On the page, these different voices emerge consecutively. But when the poem unfolds as a play of interactive energies, they arise within the larger dance of simultaneity. And we start to hear them not just in sequence, but as overtones.

Polyrhythm expresses itself both in syntactic richness and in polyphony.

50

And *this* is what I've been pressing to articulate. How technique reaches out, in desire, to recreate the polyrhythms of being.

51

Honouring polyrhythm leads to a sense of structure which is many-centred, relativist, yet open to the claim of presence. If and when it comes through.

IV · MACRO-RHYTHM

52

For decades after 1915, it seemed as though "modern poetry" and "modernist poetry" were one and the same. As though the rhythms of Pound and his peers defined the entire soundscape of a post-classical cosmos. But time has passed, and there's no need to prolong such tunnel audition.

In the 1800s, mathematicians realized that Euclidean space was not the only kind of space that could be conceived. But they didn't declare Riemann's new geometry definitive, nor Lobachevsky's, nor any other single alternative. All were legitimate, though some would prove more fruitful than others.

By the same token, it does not belittle the modernists to observe that their intuitions of a new rhythmic continuum are not the only ones that apply. Nor even, in some cases, the most fruitful. Their legacy is still staggering.

53

As a thumbnail summary:

- At the micro-scale, the creation of free-verse scoring was a seminal achievement. Syntax-and-notation may furnish the prosody of English poetry for centuries to come – as metrical prosody did in its time.

- At the mezzo-scale, the craft of compound rhythm has been largely ignored in modern poetics. But while our theories are inadequate as a result, the craft itself has been practised by modern poets in a wide variety of ways.

- At the macro-scale, the syntax of rhythm devised by Pound was that of parataxis, or discontinuous form – "vorticism," as he termed it. The basic technique was one of jump-cut ellipsis between "rhyming subjects" (in Hugh Kenner's phrase): between members of a governing analogue class. This provided an alternative to classical, linear logics for relating parts within the whole.

Pound's approach to macro-rhythm has been adopted by many modern poets, and analyzed extensively by critics. It is my conviction that as a syntax of major form, it engenders problems which it cannot resolve. However the subject is so far-reaching that I won't try to address it here.

V · POLYRHYTHMIC FORM

54

If polyrhythmic form is many-centred and relativist, it has a lot in common with the impulses of postmodernism. The latter rejects the Olympian perspective of modernism; it talks about disrupting master narratives, destabilizing unitary systems of meaning, revalorizing the margins. And that is an admirable job description.

Yet in practice I find myself restless. Not with the project itself, but with the spirit in which it is often promoted. For a great deal of its discourse goes on within a skewy ontophony.

What leads me to balk is the assumption that decentring monolithic systems is an achievement of postmodern thinkers and artists. Or that it's a human activity at all. In terms of power politics, of course, that's precisely what it is. Every authorized system renders the truths of the marginalized invisible; reclaiming those truths demands a dedicated energy of subversion. But that said, the fact is that *we* can't decentre the stories. They're already decentred. Polyrhythm precedes us; being is plural, with or without our permission. And the appropriate first response is not irony, nor even struggle, but awe. For polyrhythm is not a human creation. To think otherwise is hubris.

This blinkered ontophony has led to the shallow gamesmanship that vitiates so much postmodern poetry and fiction, and to the recombinant jargon of so much cultural theory. Its perpetual de-ing and dissing can become a refuge; it can be safer to spin theories about polyphasic meaning than to head out and try to honour its cataclysmic demands.

No recipes; no nets.

§

How to live in the here and now, with only variable meanings to go on?

You can spend your energy exposing how particular words fail to signify what is. Or you can wait upon what it is that words will always fail to signify.

56

What is rhythm?

Or rather: what are simultaneous rhythms, when none is master, privileged, normative? For the body music of world *is* many-centred. What is at issue is the nature of its relativity.

- It is reductive relativism to conclude that the truth of A is explained away or cancelled because it fails to include the truths of B and C. For B and C are inevitably subject to the same dismissal, till finally all that remains is the clever smirk of the dismisser.

- Yet we have no choice; we have to be relativist through and through. There is nothing we apprehend that doesn't get filtered through our personal temperament and cultural codes. But recognizing that has nothing to do with reductionism. Two things are true at once: we limit and distort what claims us; and we *are* claimed. Neither truth is enough without the other.

- It is polyrhythmic relativism to honour the simultaneous play of A, and B, and C. Sustained, as they are, in cadence – painfully at times, in what feels like a numinous relativity. A holy.

*

But how do you honour these jostling frequencies when fixed measures are gone? How do you enact a coherence-in-motion which is local, provisional, unstable, renewable, in-process?

By waiting, beholden, on cadence. Rich polyrhythmic manifold.

57

When you absorb rhythm kinaesthetically, the classic Western split between subject and object goes into remission.

It survives, in a weakened sense. But the old unbridgeable distance of over-against is largely bad rhythm now. Bad ontophonic grammar.

For you are not just a self-contained subject/observer – you're embedded in kinaesthetic space. And when you register its frequencies, what configures you is both outside you and within. You're a subset, a local constituent: one swatch of the plural whole. Now subject and object unclench, subside to secondary distinctions within the field.

I don't experience this as a total whiteout of ego. The local *I* goes on. But the wrench and plash and momentum go on too, and oneself is included – well before deliberate listening even begins. You could bar the door, but the walls are already down.

What is it you hear? I don't know if I'm talking about stones in a field or the sacred. All I know is, kintuition goes there. Polyrhythm is true.

58

Body music is the mind of poetry. Its rhythms think who we are, and what the world is. Not exhaustively, for there are other ways of thinking. But for real.

Kinaesthetic polyrhythm is one alternative to the impasse of modern reason – to the inability of technical thought to know the world, except by shrinking it to its own value-free categories. Polyrhythm thinks beneath the impasse, within the impasse, beyond the impasse.

*

But is it not a fresh act of hubris, to put forward a poet's experience of cadence as a paradigm of other-than-modern knowing?

Au contraire. Many kinds of witness are needed. And while this is not the only non-modern way of knowing – who will speak for it, if I don't?

Just as, if others don't tell us what *they've* been claimed by, who will?

Don McKay

The Bushtits' Nest

When I moved to the west coast from New Brunswick, bushtits were one of the first west-of-the-Rockies species I met. Unlike most such meetings, this one did not occur with my gaze flung outward through the binoculars and my body skewed – like a violinist waiting for the downbeat or a batter for the pitch – by the effort of attentiveness. In fact I was relaxing with a drink at a friend's house when they paid us a visit – a dozen or so flitting around on the branches of the Garry oaks which overhang the porch, landing on the railing, kibitzing in true titmouse style while they visibly considered our shoulders and wine glasses as possible perches. "Ah, you're the bird watcher," Rachel said, with a troubling use of the definite article, "you can tell us what these are. They always come round when we sit out here."

Of course I couldn't – which was socially embarrassing, but at the same time exciting, since the details of their presence – those flits like precise whims, the head-cock which is both curious and skeptical, the subtle grey-brown plumage (later reduced by Roger Tory Peterson to "nondescript"), their membership in a loose, chatty klatsch that seems like an idealized version of grass-roots democracy: all this could occur without the centralizing and reductive influence of the name, which so often signals the terminal point of our interest. "Ah, bushtits": check, snap. Next topic.

But naming has its indisputable satisfactions. To find bushtits later in the bird guide, to fit them ("I *knew* it") into the titmouse family along with chickadees of every stripe and cap: this is one of the pleasures of system to which us big brains are addicted. We aren't (certainly I wasn't) willing to remain on the phenomenological edge for very long before that itch to identify things, to place them taxonomically, kicks in. I'd hesitate to say that satisfactions of naming are erotic ones, but they certainly come with the sense of a compulsion relieved – akin to smoking, maybe, or finding a washroom when the call is urgent. And knowing the name leads to other tidbits of knowledge: for instance that southwestern B.C. is the northern extremity of their range; that they are songless (meaning, really, that their twittering *recitative* covers the function of territory and breeding managed by a separate song in other species); and that they weave elaborate hanging nests like hairy gourds – larger and more intricate than a northern oriole's, complete with a side entrance and a roof.

I have access to all these wonders because I have passed through the strait gate of nomenclature. Of course, the field guides and reference books usually convey information in terse asyntactical bursts of fact and like to think of themselves as clinically awe-free. But the pose is pretty thin, and wears through entirely in their frequent recourse to metaphor, often, interestingly, when attempting descriptions of songs and calls. A Swainson thrush's call note ("whoit") is the sound of a drop of water in a barrel; a rose-breasted grosbeak sounds like a robin who has been taking singing lessons. And that move into mini-poem, far from being an aberration, is often the point of greatest descriptive accuracy, when a sure sense of the song (flight, nest, whatever) is conveyed. If you're like me, that is also the point that's likely to stick in memory, long after the dates and measurements have abandoned the premises.

But I want to claim something more for these metaphorical moments, having to do with their energy, with the sheer muscle required to speak a lie in the interests of truth, and leap between two distant regions of experience. One metaphor for the excitement of metaphors is to say they are entry points where wilderness re-invades language, the place where words put their authority at risk, implicitly confessing their inadequacy to the task of representing the world. Their very excess points to a world beyond language, even while it cuts a fancy linguistic figure. They are our route back to that live, still nameless birdlet who is checking out the half-recumbent drinkers on the porch, one flit away from taking an experimental sip of my Sauvignon Blanc.

*

Is there any paradox more telling, more reverberant and carrying in its gesture, than the one set in motion by the first lines of the *Tao Te Ching*?

> *The tao that can be told*
> *is not the eternal Tao.*
> *The name that can be named*
> *is not the eternal Name.*
> (Trans. Stephen Mitchell)

At the outset, this disclaimer about the ability of language to do the job: it can be no more than – in the traditional metaphor – a finger pointing at the moon.

And there is also the legend of how the *Tao Te Ching* came to be written, adding the charm and acoustical dwell of anecdote. Lao-tzu, having lived for a long time in the country of Chou, was leaving. The border guard, realizing this was his last chance to consult the sage, asked for a book to teach him the way. So Lao-tzu wrote the *Tao Te Ching,* gave it to the border guard, and left.

I think about this scene quite a bit: not only the sage leaving for what I think of as wilderness – the placeless place beyond the mind's appropriations, and not only the great poem written and immediately let go; I also think of that border guard with his divided being, guarding the frontier while revering the sage whose teachings point beyond it. I think his situation quite resembles the poet's – or at least the nature poet's. Whatever her admiration for wilderness, she remains a citizen of the frontier, a creature of words who will continue to use them to point – sometimes at the moon, sometimes simply at the figure of the departed sage. A poem, or poem-in-waiting, contemplates what language can't do: then it does something with language – in homage, or grief, or anger, or praise.

*

One writes because one has been touched by the yearning for and despair of ever touching the Other.
 (Charles Simic, in *The Poet's Notebook*)

*

Naturally, one thinks of superb moments in lyric poetry as the entry points of wilderness. But even institutional language sometimes stumbles into a forlorn eloquence, possibly because the level of appropriation is so extreme that wilderness is made conspicuous, and vocal, by its absence. Most of us could point to a few suburbs and malls whose burlesque of 'natural' phenomena is classic; sometimes they're named after the very White Oaks or crystal creeks lost or compromised in their construction. I was thinking along these lines while driving in the back country of southern Vancouver Island, where – as elsewhere – the logging road often takes its name from the creek or river that has, over ten thousand years or so, cut a pass into hills and provided the road with access to the cutblocks. So if you're travelling on the Mosquito Creek Main or Harris Creek Main, you should be prepared for some fairly dismal views of the creek so named. They may also be views that are only too unobstructed, since the avowed practice of leaving a substantial fringe of trees along water courses as a stay against erosion seems to be more often ignored than honoured. Perhaps the most extreme case of such eloquence in my experience is Jordan River Main, partly because of its echo of the sacred river of the holy land, and partly because the river is – for a good portion of its length – gone. Jordan River has been dammed to generate electrical power and sent, first underground through a tunnel beneath the ridge, then overland through a penstock which crawls through a clear cut area (where it looks like a leftover prop from an extremely low budget sci-fi flick about cosmic worms) before it is finally discharged through the turbines and allowed to flow out into the Strait of Juan de Fuca. Matériel. So views of Jordan River from Jordan River Main or Jordan River East Main are in fact views of the basaltic boulders which were once its bed. Name as epitaph.

*

A SMALL FABLE

It had been a long hard day, but he had performed perfectly, a parade of A-pluses. Every suggestion he made had been endorsed 100% by his proud parent, and set instantly in bronze. But that night he woke up troubled. The shadow of doubt which had lent just the right dark note to the noontide ceremony, the hint of a minor key, had now become the prevailing mood. Adam played over his choices – otter, egret, archaeopteryx, columbine, yellow warbler, zebra – trying to recall that immense mid-day satisfaction, that sense of an inexorable order inexorably ordering, as though his Father's gaze had simply entered the creature to gaze back. "Onion," said the onions; "Trumpeter swan," said the Trumpeter swans; "Enchanter's nightshade," said the Enchanter's nightshades with – was that the suggestion of a smirk? Surely not. But now Adam was not so sure he hadn't missed something, some slippage in the belts and snaps, a little play between "Cooper's hawk" and the bird with the fierce orange eye and the talons like sharpened knitting needles. It bothered him; he got up and began to prowl around the bower, fidgeting, plucking at the odd fig leaf, his mind already hatching the idea of a cigarette and a cup of coffee.

From outside came a sad shaking of the air, a small whinny which Adam knew to be the voice of the screech owl he had named at 4:37 that afternoon. *Screech* owl? What had he been thinking? Obviously by 4:30 his edge was off and it had been clear that his Father would endorse any old label just to keep things, as He liked to say, on sched. Now Adam could see – or rather hear – what a bonehead of a name it was. Anyone could tell you that a screech was an *ascending* scream: his mind flashed forward to a '58 Pontiac Bonneville braking, *screeching* into the rending metal crash and tinkling of glass which followed. But the owl's voice fluttered down, a heart sinking, it went down like – Adam paused, finger to lips – like a little aluminum ladder. Bingo. This was more like it: "the little aluminum ladder of its scream." Adam loved its riskiness, its resonance, the way it connected something airy with the world of tools and – incredibly – found common ground. How it made the etched, metallic quality of the owl's call come forward; how it made the ladder into an act. The resonances just kept oscillating, unlike "screech owl," which just sat there, glum, a cage for the bird which could be set down in one place or another in the sentence. Adam thought of calling his Father to propose a revision, but he could already hear the note of disapproval in His voice at the suggestion of spending six words on what was after all one of Creation's smaller owls. Adam remembered His stern gaze, His dislike of shilly-shallying, His love of code.

By this time sleep had withdrawn for the night (so recently separated from the day) and Adam was thoroughly agitated. He recalled his nominations with a new critical eye and ear, feeling their clunkiness, their prefab quality: ring-necked duck, common loon: they lay there like shucked cocoons. He walked outside, and down the path toward the woods. Most things were shapes that loomed or withdrew into pools of darkness, and nothing wore the label it had been given that afternoon. Was that red oak? Was that silver maple? Adam approached, hoping to embrace a trunk, and got jabbed just below the eye by a stiff twig covered in needles. "Black spruce" he remembered, quickly amending to "bristling boreal arms." Would the whole ceremony have to be done again under the moon's changing eye? Would everything have to have a day name and a night name?

Suddenly he felt, rather than saw or heard, a stirring as a presence flew past him, a darker darkness that swept down the path and into the foliage, leaving a little whinny hanging. That was "little aluminum ladder of its scream" alright, but now Adam realized that the new name, much though it improved on "screech owl," did nothing for that gentle fatal presence on the path, that extra hush he had lived with for a moment. It was as if – Adam groped inwardly as he made his way back to the bower, holding the quality of the experience in his mind as though cradling an egg. It was as if....

Would it be later that night, or the next day, or very much later after sex and the fall, that he'd finally name that presence on the path as the little sister of death? Or would that be one of those that never came to words?

*

His beak could open a bottle,
and his eyes – when he lifts their soft lids –
go on reading something
just beyond your shoulder –
Blake, maybe,
or the Book of Revelation.

Never mind that he eats only
the black-smocked crickets,
and dragonflies if they happen
to be out late over the ponds, and of course
the occasional festal mouse.
Never mind that he is only a memo
from the offices of fear –

> *it's not size but surge that tells us*
> *when we're in touch with something real,*
> *and when I hear him in the orchard*
> *fluttering*
> *down the little aluminum ladder of his scream —*
> (from Mary Oliver's
> "Little Owl Who Lives in the Orchard")

*

The *duende* of Lorca: a violent upsurge of the other inside language and art — the arrival of chthonic force with its irrationality, its earthiness, its message that death is just *there,* at your elbow; the dread connection to wilderness along the dark artery of our common mortality. And the 'animal music' of Ted Hughes, that vestige of shamanic power in poetry which can "make the spirits listen," and can, unless regulated and domesticated by the forms of art, induce madness.

With idea, sound, or gesture, the duende enjoys fighting the creator on the very rim of the well. Angel and muse escape with violin, meter and compass; the duende wounds. In the healing of that wound, which never closes, lie the strange, invented qualities of a man's work.
(Federico García Lorca, "Play and Theory of the Duende")

And Hughes:

> *Like that cry within the sea,*
> *A mumbling over and over*
> *Of ancient law, the phrasing falling to pieces*
> *Garbled among shell-shards and gravels,*
>   *the truths falling to pieces,*

> *The sea pulling everything to pieces*
> *Except its killers, alert and shapely*
> (from "Logos")

What a contrast to the crossings recommended and demonstrated by the Taoist sages! In the exercise of spontaneity, or the knack which animates craft (cooking, pottery, archery, music), the border simply vanishes and wilderness, unfettered by consciousness, expresses itself.

> *The poem makes itself*
> *when it is ready and the poet*
> *Light-hearted enough in his grief*
> *or good fortune*
>
> *In the valley below Filloti*
> *we had our lunch under an oak tree,*
> *the wind blowing the paper on*
> *which I cut bread*
> (John Steffler, "Wind")

*

Culture can, first, be interpreted ... as an intention to remove the otherness of Nature, which, alien and previous, surprises and strikes the immediate identity that is the Same of the human self.
(Emmanuel Levinas, "The Philosophical Determination of the Idea of Culture," *Entre Nous*)

It is the legacy of Emmanuel Levinas' thought that we should be able to contemplate the other as a fundamental category, to dislodge our usual assumptions about the primacy of such things as sameness, selfhood, ego, being and totality. No less than Lorca or Hughes, Levinas realizes how the self defends its identity against incursions of wilderness (the 'alien and previous' otherness of Nature) by the complicated apparatus of culture, which works to reinforce those very assumptions. But this set of centralizing tendencies leads both to the distortion of reality and to the related political evils of totality. The contrary idea of wholeness, with otherness kept scrupulously in mind, Levinas calls infinity.

For Levinas, ethics – which we might summarize as the calling-into-question of our freedom to control, process, or reduce the other – should be 'first philosophy'; that is, it is with ethics, and not ontology (as with Heidegger) that we should begin our attempts to understand the world. Heidegger, in whose philosophy Levinas was initially immersed, had proposed ontology – the philosophy of being – as first philosophy, itself replacing or "overcoming" the metaphysics which, Heidegger claimed, had dominated western philosophy since Aristotle.

And Heidegger is also known for what seems at first glance to be the excellent advice that we should 'let beings be,' rather than reducing them to the status of 'standing reserve,' as, for example, cut-blocks or kidnapped rivers. But Levinas calls this into question. Is it sufficient simply to leave the other alone, to take a hands-off position?

Is our relation to the other a letting be*? Is not the independence of the other achieved through his or her rôle as one who is addressed? Is the person to whom we speak understood beforehand in his being? Not at all. The other is not first an object of understanding and then an interlocutor. The two relations are merged. In other words, addressing the other is inseparable from understanding the other.*

("Is Ontology Fundamental?," *Entre Nous*)

A person might be reminded here of Wittgenstein's remark that meaning is going up to someone. This view of the importance of *address* to the other (as opposed to passivity or 'letting beings be'), with its implication that the gesture acknowledges a responsibility, a limitation of the freedom of beings in favour of the other, reaches a point of dramatic focus in Levinas' concept of the Face.

What Levinas means by the Face is, I think, the other encountered in a relationship of address as quite untranslatable into systems of sameness and linguistic organization; it is foreign-ness that remains foreign, always exceeding our categories of knowing, always "over and beyond form" (*Totality and Infinity*). It seems to be a far more nuanced, philosophically literate and conceptually far-reaching version of what I've been calling wilderness, as this expresses itself in poetic attention.

But a problem presents itself – at least for me – and, interestingly, it is a problem of nomenclature. To personify the untranslated other as the Face seems, in fact, to translate it into terms which are, if not exclusively human, at least restricted to members of the 'higher' animal kingdom, shutting out such creatures as Douglas-fir, waves and clams, to say nothing of lichens, rocks and chairs. Its strength lies in its appeal to the experience we often have of 'putting a face' to another person, or 'recognizing' the rights and values of a minority group. It is easier, probably even for a Texas governor, to kill an abstract criminal on death row than a person whose face one has seen in photographs or the flesh. But in its apparent anthropocentrism (or vertobratocentrism?), the Face initially seems an inadequate term for any non-animal other we might truly address.

But further reflection may reveal, as it did for me, something of the wisdom of Levinas' choice. Anthropocentrism, in Walt Disney films or plans for wildlife management, is clearly an evil we wish to avoid. But when we take stock of our situation as language users with brains and organs of perception which dictate that we see and describe the world in human ways, we can see that, at bottom, a human perspective is impossible to avoid. Though we may devote attention to the screech owl or the cat-tail moss, we are inevitably translators of their being, at least when we come to representation. "Isn't art," Levinas asks rhetorically, "an activity that gives things a face?" Even an artist like Cézanne, whose work, as Merleau-Ponty puts it, renders a perspective "from below the imposed order of humanity" as if "viewed by a creature of another species," has not truly managed to escape the perspectival cage. He is still daubing pigment on stretched canvas, as no other species has been known to do.

So here's how I'm reading the Face: it's an address to the other with an acknowledgement of our human-centredness built in, a salutary and humbling reminder. But we can perform artistic acts in such a way that, in 'giving things a face,' the emphasis falls on the gift, the way, for example, a linguistic community might honour a stranger by conferring upon her a name in their language. Homage is, perhaps, simply appropriation with the current reversed; 'here,' we say to the thing, 'is a tribute from our culture, in which having a face is the premier sign of status.' We can, in short, try to be like Cézanne rather than Mount Rushmore.

*

STOOL

In the end one cannot keep this love concealed
tiny quadruped with oaken legs
o skin coarse and fresh beyond expression
everyday object eyeless but with a face
on which the wrinkles of the grain mark a ripe judgement
grey little mule most patient of mules
its hair has fallen out from too much fasting
and only a tuft of wooden bristle
can my hand feel when I stroke it in the morning

– Do you know my darling they were charlatans
who said: the hand lies the eye
lies when it touches shapes that are empty –

they were bad people envious of things
they wanted to trap the world with the bait of denial

how to express to you my gratitude wonder
you come always to the call of the eye
with great immobility explaining by dumb-signs
to a sorry intellect: we are genuine –
At last the fidelity of things opens our eyes
   (Zbigniew Herbert, trans. Czesław Miłosz
   and Peter Dale Scott)

*

Envisaging rather than naming: to bring in all that a face presents – character, expression, imagination, mobility of feature, traces of the past in lines and crowfeet. A face is a face is a face; it is not primarily a linguistic being whose chief virtue is ease of manipulation. And when a lake or a pine marten looks back, when we are – however momentarily – *vis à vis,* the pause is always electric. Are we not right to sense, in such meetings, that envisaging flows both ways?

*

> How the slash looks: not
> ruin, abattoir, atrocity;
> not harvest, regen, working
> forest. How it looks. The way it
> keeps on looking when we look away,
> embarrassed. How it gawks,
> with no nuance or subterfuge
> or shadow. How it seems to see us now
> as we see it. Not quick.
> Not dead.

*

Last spring, while out watching for returning warblers in a local park, I came upon a pair of bushtits building their nest. Actually, I didn't realize what they were doing right off: it seemed like some sort of bonding ritual in which each of them buzzed from the surrounding trees into this one open space at the top of a dogwood shrub, fluttered a moment, then buzzed out again. Unlike their usual flitterings, these flights were filled with intent, aimed. Eventually I was able to make out something in that space, some slight thickening of air, if it wasn't one of those gauzy jellyfish-like floaters that can occur in your vision due to some momentary aberration inside your eyeball. The bushtits were – as I inferred later with the help of reference books – probably just beginning to attach leaf matter and lichens to the spider web they use for struts and girders (and which apparently has tensile strength greater than steel), but to me it looked like their flitterings were an attempt to summon something out of nothing, preparing the air for some sudden incarnation. When I went back the next day the nest already had the consistency of a string bag or a cloud of algae, and its gourd shape was visible. The bushtits continued to buzz in and out, only now I could see the occasional bit of twig or leaf in their beaks, and they would land on one of the adjacent branches before tucking the new bit into the nest-in-progress.

*

In this passage, it is useful to remember that for the ancient Chinese, the heart is the organ of thought.

> — *I venture to enquire about the fasting of the heart.*
> — *Unify your attention. Rather than listen with the ear, listen with the heart. Rather than listen with the heart, listen with the energies. Listening stops at the ear, the heart at what tallies with the thought. As for energy* [chi] *it is the tenuous which waits to be roused by other things. Only the Way accumulates the tenuous. The attenuating is the fasting of the heart.*
> (Chuang-tzu, *The Seven Inner Chapters*, trans. A.C. Graham)

*

To be next door to nothing: it's not only their nests, but the bushtits themselves that convey this paradoxical power. They are 'creatures of the air' not only because they fly through it, but because it comprises so much of their bodily presence. All birds, in fact, live close to the edge. Typically, they draw air into sacs throughout their bodies, and even, in some cases, into their hollow bones.

They also expel all the air from the lungs with each exhalation, without holding back, as we do, a reserve. Nor do they put on fat they aren't about to burn up in migration. Birds do not need a Lao-tzu to remind them of the non-being their lives depend on.

*

It was a while after I observed the bushtits in the park that I noticed a similar busy-ness in the forsythia bush which hangs over our driveway. Sure enough, another pair had chosen this improbable space eighteen inches over a Toyota Corolla, with its door slams and exhaust, its big blocky comings and goings, as the site of their future home. I think the forsythia's tangle of twigs and branches may have appealed to them as stabilizers coming to the assistance of spider webs. At first, I was careful not to park in the driveway for fear of disturbing them, but – having forgotten once or twice – it soon became apparent that the bushtits' idea of home was closer to a kitchen in Newfoundland than to a hermitage. The car didn't bother them, and neither, it seemed, did our curiosity, which – after all – seemed to echo theirs.

Now, eight months later, the bushtits have long since raised their chicks and left, but the forsythia tangle still holds this gathered thickness inside it, looking like a vital organ. It is easy to stand in the driveway and inspect it close up – an infinity of tucks and weavings worked in grasses, mosses and lichens. Cat-tail moss seems to have been especially useful for its feather boa-like length and softness, and so has one of the beard lichens (*Usnea subfloridana?*) which has a strong central cord like a tendon running through it. I think the lichens came largely from our neighbour's wood fence, where at least four species grow in profusion, and where I have often seen bushtits perching – briefly – in a pause between flits.

Since moving to B.C. and meeting a bona fide lichenologist in the person of Trevor Goward, I've become aware of just how abundant and amazing these overlooked beings are. That is not the sort of awareness anyone who meets Trevor is likely to escape, since his commitment to 'the spread of enlichenment,' as he puts it, is intense. He would certainly want it noted that the bushtits have been engaged in the reproduction of lichens while they are busy about reproduction of their own, since those lichens that do not spread through spores rely on the transportation of bits of their thalluses (bodies) by birds. But more fundamentally, he would want us to realize that a lichen is a very complex life form, the visible consequence of a symbiotic relationship between a fungus and microscopic algae. Lichens are, in Trevor's memorable and – at least among the enlichened – famous metaphor, fungi that have discovered agriculture.

I remember reading that phrase in the lichen section of *Plants in Coastal British Columbia* before I met its author, and being immediately engaged. Thinking back to that experience will provide a convenient place to end (though not to conclude), since it returns us to the scene of naming and envisaging we've been busily flitting around, tucking and weaving. Besides the elegance of Trevor's metaphor, and the efficiency with which it does the job of informing, we should notice the implied homage or gift that the gesture makes: to see lichens as fungi who practice agriculture is to see them in the same light that we conceive our own passage, as human beings, from the raw to the cooked, and to confer on them some of the value and acclaim we usually reserve for things human. And while we're paused there, mildly agog at the prospect of domestication occurring in the natural world, let's also take in the pure pizzazz of the metaphorical act releasing another micro-quantum of wild figuration into the body of language – that tiny, shocking, necessary invasion; that saving of language from itself.

SOURCES

(*in order of appearance*)

Tao Te Ching, trans. Stephen Mitchell. New York: Harper & Row, 1988.

Kuusisto, Stephen, et al, ed. *The Poet's Notebook: Excerpts from the Notebooks of Contemporary American Poets.* New York: Norton, 1995.

Oliver, Mary. "Little Owl Who Lives in the Orchard." *New and Selected Poems.* Boston: Beacon Press, 1992.

García Lorca, Federico. "Play and Theory of the Duende," trans. Christopher Maurer. *In Search of Duende.* New York: New Directions, 1998.

Hughes, Ted. "Logos." *Wodwo.* London: Faber & Faber, 1967.

Steffler, John. "Wind." *That Night We Were Ravenous.* Toronto: McClelland & Stewart, 1998.

Levinas, Emmanuel. *Entre Nous,* trans. Michael B. Smith and Barbara Harshav. London: Athlone, 1998.

Merleau-Ponty, Maurice. "Cézanne's Doubt." *The Essential Merleau-Ponty,* ed. Alden Fisher. New York: Harcourt Brace, 1969.

Herbert, Zbigniew. "Stool." *Selected Poems,* trans. Czesław Miłosz and Peter Dale Scott. New York: Ecco Press, 1986.

Chuang-tzu. *The Seven Inner Chapters and Other Writings,* trans. A.C. Graham. London: George Allen & Unwin, 1981.

Robert Bringhurst

The Philosophy of Poetry and the Trashing of Doctor Empedokles

HISTORIANS, LIKE PHYSICISTS, are free to change their metaphors and minds – free to say on Tuesday, "These are the inarguable facts" and on Thursday free to say the facts have changed or must be seen in a new light. They say today that a Greek philosopher named Empedokles was born in the 490s BCE, perhaps on the southwest coast of Sicily. Hölderlin and Matthew Arnold, who can change their minds no more, say that he died of his own choice, diving into molten rock in the crater of Mt Etna.

Together with Parmenides, Empedokles also heads the rather long list of authors who, like Rabelais, Campion, Chekhov, Benn, Céline, and William Carlos Williams, were licensed in their time to practise as physicians. Dante, Keats and Trakl were licensed as pharmacists instead. There are not, in the history of poetry, any licensed poets, nor in the history of philosophy any licensed metaphysicians, but there are doctors, lawyers, hunters, farmers, school teachers, monks and Indian chiefs. Poetry and thinking are vocations, not professions.

Empedokles may have been born in the same year as Sophocles. Read in that light, his poetry may always seem comparatively narrow, raw and pale. But poetry is what it seems to be. I think we miss the boat if we regard him as merely an early cosmologist – and one whose work is twice unblessed, being not only in fragments but *versified*.

He is one of the three canonical Presocratic thinkers who composed in Greek hexameters rather than prose, and for that even poets have made him pay. T.S. Eliot lumps together two of the three, Empedokles and Parmenides, as "apparently persons of an impure philosophical inspiration" and "persons who mingled with genuine philosophical ability a good deal of the emotion of the founder of a second-rate religious system."[1] That is a judgement as harsh in its way as Quevedo's, for whom Empedokles is *descubrióse por juez y legislador…, hombre tan desatinado, que afirmando que había sido pez*: "a self-appointed legislator and judge…, a man so daft that he insisted he'd been a fish."[2] In a later age, the most sober and serious biologists have told us we have all been fish and could not be humans otherwise.

I am not sure, myself, that anyone is ever "the founder of a second-rate religious system." Religious systems seem to me mostly products of their followers. And if we substitute "follower" for "founder" in Eliot's formulation, then his put-down can be readily applied to any philosopher or any thinking poet whose ideas about the nature of reality or the rightness of certain actions happen to differ from our own. Eliot himself could fall into this category in many people's minds. But Aristotle's claim, that Empedokles was a versifier rather than a poet, underlies Eliot's dismissal, and it is a charge we had better review.

The accusation comes in the opening pages of Aristotle's *Poetics* (§1447b):

καὶ γὰρ ἂν ἰατρικόν ἢ φυσικόν τι διὰ τῶν μέτρων ἐκφέρωσιν, οὕτω καλεῖν εἰώθασιν· οὐδὲν δὲ κοινόν ἐστιν Ὁμήρῳ καὶ Ἐμπεδοκλεῖ

πλὴν τὸ μέτρον, διὸ τὸν μὲν ποιητὴν δίκαινον καλεῖν, τὸν δὲ φυσιο-
λόγον μᾶλλον ἢ ποιητήν· ὁμοίως δὲ κἂν εἴ τις ἅπαντα τὰ μέτρα
μιγνύων ποιοῖτο τὴν μίμησιν καθάπερ Χαιρήμων ἐποίησε Κέν-
ταυρον μικτὴν ῥαψῳδίαν ἐξ ἁπάντων τῶν μέτρων, καὶ ποιητὴν
προσαγορευτέον. περὶ μὲν οὖν τούτων διωρίσθω τοῦτον τὸν τρόπον.

Even when someone addresses the subject of medicine or natural science in verse, it is usual to call him by the same term [poet]. Homer and Empedokles have only their scansion in common, so in fact it would be proper to call one of them a poet, the other one a naturalist [φυσιολόγος] rather than a poet [ποιητής]. In the same way, when someone makes a stew of different meters, as Khairemon did in his Centaur — a medley of every sort of verse form — he is generally referred to as a "poet." That's enough of such distinctions.

In the *Metaphysics* (985a), where clarity, not poetry, is the subject under discussion, Aristotle scoffs all the harder at his predecessor:

εἰ γάρ τις ἀκολουθοίη καὶ λαμβάνοι πρὸς τὴν διάνοιαν καὶ μὴ
πρὸς ἃ ψελλίζεται λέγων Ἐμπεδοκλῆς....

If a person were to stalk and trap the underlying thought, not the faltering speech, of Empedokles....

It is, if not stupid, at least presumptuous to argue this with Aristotle. He had much more of Empedokles' work than we have on which to base a judgement. He also had a grasp of classical Greek and a knowledge of its literature which no one now can match. But at the same time, we have access to a great deal of poetry, and to many whole literatures, and genres and species of literature, which Aristotle, writing just a century after Empedokles, could not know anything about. I at any rate am ill-equipped to question Aristotle's judgement, yet I am forced all the same to form new judgements of my own. So the fact that we have Empedokles (and Parmenides and Herakleitos) in fragments is as important to me in its way as the fact that Aristotle had them more or less whole. No matter what respect we owe to Aristotle's views on the Presocratics, it is useless just to parrot them; it is also hard – because of what has happened to the evidence and of what has happened to *us* – to share them very deeply. If we are going to think anything at all about the work of Empedokles, we have to think it on the basis of the fragments that survive. And on the basis of those fragments, Empedokles looks, to me at least, a lot more like a poet than Aristotle (or Eliot) would lead us to believe.

In another essay, Eliot tells us that two poets he feels closer to, Ben Jonson and George Chapman,

were notably men who incorporated their erudition into their sensibility: their mode of feeling was directly and freshly altered by their reading and thought. In Chapman especially there is a direct and sensuous apprehension of thought, or a recreation of thought into feeling, which is exactly what we find in Donne.[3]

These are interesting assertions. One way of testing just how interesting they are is to subject them to some trial transformations.

I can try to read Empedokles, Parmenides and Herakleitos purely as philosophers. If I do so, I keep sensing all the same that they lean toward poetry or are tainted by it in some way. Is it possible, for example, that they are describable in just the terms Eliot uses in speaking of Jonson and Chapman? Or perhaps in just the opposite terms? It's worth a try. Suppose we say that these three Presocratics *were notably men who incorporated their sensibility into their erudition: their mode of thought was directly and freshly altered by their feeling. In Parmenides especially there is a direct intellectual apprehension of sensation, or a recreation of feeling into thought, which is exactly what we find in* ... well, in Heidegger, in Kierkegaard, in Wittgenstein, in Nietzsche, often in Pascal.

It would be easy enough to say the same of many poets: of Dante and Cavalcanti, for example, of John Davies and John Donne, of Joyce and Eliot and Pound, and more notably of Mallarmé and Rilke. And it might not be too difficult to apply Eliot's uninverted statement to certain philosophers: Ortega, for example.

A certain school of critics has taught for many years that form and content ought to coincide, attaining what scholastic thinkers called *circumincession*. In much of the best twentieth-century writing, as in much of the best poetry since Dante (or, in English, since Shakespeare and Donne), there is such a circumincession, a "mutual indwelling," not of form and content but rather of feeling and thought. In fact, that achievement is the subject of many of Donne's poems. It is clearly the method as well as the substance of many poems written in more recent times. (There is a sense, perhaps, in which it really is the method of all poems.) Donne thought the thought came first, though Eliot says that Donne worked by the opposite method. Learning to hold neither view and both may be much healthier than choosing.

Still, I want to know whether "philosophical poetry" is a useful term, and whether it has something to do with Empedokles. The attempt at a "philosophical poem" could fail, I suppose, in either or both of two ways. It could fail to yield poetry, in which case what remained might or might not still be philosophy. Or it could fail to be "philosophical," in which case what remained might or might not continue to be poetry: might or might not lapse into poetry of some other kind. In Empedokles' extant fragments the repetitive failure – which is no failure at all – is of the second sort. The poetry keeps slipping out of philosophy and not vice versa; the poetry is continually taking control. Frequently, indeed, the poetry (I do not mean the verse) seems to waft the thought along more than to fuse with it. Empedokles is no Donne, and no Cavalcanti. But the verse is an issue. The Greek hexameter, bred for narrative, is not a form that will carry all the cadences of human intellection. Parmenides made it work for a kind of philosophy, but the hard core of Sophocles' thought – that is to say, the hard core of his poetry – takes the form of "free verse." Often this "freedom" is disguised. Sophocles often pairs serious strophe with lighter antistrophe to achieve the choral song. In his work, ideas dance and sing. That if anything ought to be what we mean by philosophical poetry. Still, what about Empedokles? Is he really "philosophical" at all, in more than a rudimentary sense of the term?

One of the species of thought which *is* frequently present in Empedokles and Sophocles alike might be called reflection rather than philosophy. It is to be found in many writers both of poetry and prose. Empedokles discussing how his four basic elements interact, for example, is reminiscent of this passage from Thoreau:

It seems natural that rocks which have lain under the heavens so long should be gray, as it were an intermediate color between the heavens and the earth. The air is the thin paint in which they have been dipped and brushed with the wind. Water, which is more fluid and like the sky in its nature, is still more like it in color. Time will make the most discordant materials harmonize....

This is reflection, or meditation, or rumination; it is also celebration. In the loose sense of the word, it is "philosophical." I am not sure what we gain, though, by calling it philosophy. Nor would I claim that it is a great example of poetry. Neither are the corresponding passages in Empedokles' Greek. But what about a passage such as this one (DK fragment 105)?

*αἵματος ἐν πελάγεσσι τεθραμμένη ἀντιθρόντος
τῆι τε νόημα μάλιστα κικλήσκεται ἀνθρώποισιν·
αἷμα γὰρ ἀνθρώποις περικάρδιόν ἐστι νόημα.*

*... tumbling in the surf and undertow
of blood, where the thing called thought is. Thought
is, in fact, the blood around the human heart.*

That is an image which, after two and a half millennia, and after all the anatomical researches of Galen, Servetus and William Harvey, still gets my attention. There are other fragments – DK 62 is an example – not made obsolete by Darwin or by Leakey:

*νῦν δ' ἄγ' ὅπως ἀνδρῶν τε πολυκλαύτων τε γυναικῶν
ἐννυχίους ὅρπηκας ἀνήγαγε κρινόμενον πῦρ,
τῶνδε κλῦ'· οὐ γὰρ μῦθος ἀπόσκοπος οὐδ' ἀδαήμων.
οὐλοφυεῖς μὲν πρῶτα τύποι χθονὸς ἐξανέτελλον,
ἀμφοτέρων ὕδατός τε καὶ εἴδεος αἶσαν ἔχοντες·
τοὺς μὲν πῦρ ἀνέπεμπε θέλον πρὸς ὁμοῖον ἱκέσθαι,
οὔτε τί πω μελέων ἐρατὸν δέμας ἐμφαίνοντας,
οὔτ' ἐνοπὴν οὔτ' αὖ ἐπιχώριον ἀνδράσι γυῖον.*

*This is how the fire, as it separated, germinated
the night-flowering seedlings of human beings. Listen.
The lesson is relevant and full of information. Listen.
Crooked forms imprinted out of earth existed first. They
were partly water and partly opaque shape. Fire
desired to arrive at its own image, that's why fire
forced them into flower. They didn't yet have attractive limbs
nor the hand and the lonely voice which fuse in a man.*

Then there are fragments such as this (DK 57):

ἧι πολλαὶ μὲν κόρσαι ἀναύχενες ἐβλάστησαν.
γυμνοὶ δ' ἐπλάζοντο βραχίονες εὔνιδες ὤμων,
ὄμματα τ' οἶ' ἐπλανᾶτο πενηιεύοντα μετώπων....

*Maxillae went into motion without mandibles,
arms walked naked, unhinged from their shoulders,
eyeballs wandered without brows....*

This is not philosophy; it is surrealism: one of the most ancient and widespread of all artistic modes. Horace, more than four centuries later, was familiar with many examples. He begins his longest poem, the *Ars poetica,* trying to make himself look good at their expense:

```
humano capiti ceruicem pictor equinam
iungere si uelit, et uarias inducere plumas
undique collatis membris, ut turpiter atrum
desinat in piscem mulier formosa superne,
spectatum admissi risum teneatis, amici?
credite, Pisones, isti tabulae fore librum
persimilem, cuius, uelut aegri somnia, uanae
fingentur species....
```

> *A human head, a horse's neck: suppose a painter puts the two*
> *together, and attaches many different kinds of feathers*
> *to the body parts he picks up here and there,*
> *or grafts a fine-looking woman's upper body*
> *to the hindparts of a limp, discolored fish.*
> *Friends, could you keep your laughter back*
> *if you saw such a show? Let me tell you, though,*
> *Pisos, that a book would be as silly as those pictures*
> *if the sentences were modeled on a sick man's dreams....*

Horace isn't making fun of Salvador Dalí or Tzara or Breton. He is thumbing his Roman nose at Empedokles, who is named, after much delay, at the end of the poem.

I don't know if Horace ever learned, in later life, to read Empedokles. I don't know whether Eliot did either, but I know that he continued to think about the relationship of poetry and philosophy, and that his thinking continued to mature. Some years after the essay on Dante, from which I have quoted, he addressed himself to the Metaphysical Poets. It may be wrong to speak of Cowley, Donne and Chapman as philosopher-poets, but they are poets who knew that the mind is a sensory organ like the eye, and for whom there was no aesthetic experience more satisfying than thinking. They are also poets more congenial to Eliot than the Presocratics ever were. They helped him take a larger view:

A philosophical theory which has entered into poetry is established, for its truth or falsity in one sense ceases to matter, and its truth in another sense is proved.[4]

The work of Empedokles is evidence that the same thing can be true of medical and physical hypotheses.

Insofar as they are poetry, they are permanent. Empedokles has not rewritten his work since Aristotle's classification of him as "physical scientist rather than poet," but some of his fragments either always were or have now become poems. No doubt there have been losses on the other side. The works of Hesiod may have lost whatever poetry they once contained. So perhaps has the *Henriade* of Voltaire. And Bishop Grosseteste's verse treatise on animal husbandry, if it ever was a poem, does not seem to be one now. The boundaries of the mundane and the prosaic are not eternally fixed. And the boundaries of poetry? Are they perpetually advancing and retreating, in the scuffle of little platoons of the avant-garde? Things move without moving. The town of Akragas, where Empedokles once taught, is now Agrigento and Porto Empédocle: Italian, not Greek. Its size and its shape and its language have changed. Which of its coordinates are fixed? In the case of Empedokles' poems, the change is in part due to erosion. If his work were intact, like the work of Thucydides, it might still be successfully defended by the partisans of prose – or the partisans of poetry might refuse it.

The scraps of literary gossip that survive tell us that Empedokles wrote at least two substantial works, *Peri physeos* and *Katharmoi*. Neither was anywhere near the size of the *Odyssey* or *Paradise Lost,* but both were book-length poems in the modern sense, approaching the length of, say, *A Draft of XXX Cantos*. In that case, they were works big enough to allow and demand a periodic flattening of tone. The fragments which survive are not passages chosen by Matthew Arnold as touchstones; they are bits picked to illustrate points in philosophy, theology, or natural science. Some of them are quoted by admirers – Simplikios, for example. Others are quoted by antagonists such as Hippolytos of Rome, an early third-century bishop who set himself the task of tracing Christian heresies to the teachings of pagan philosophers – and thereby helped to save their work. Suppose, for comparison, that someone were to raid Pound's work, taking only the lines which invite reinsertion into a history of China or a study of monetary theory. What if nothing remained of St-John Perse except extracts chosen to ornament a treatise on textiles or a textbook of geography?

The Empedokles who composed the full texts of *Peri physeos* and *Katharmoi* is unknown to us and must, I guess, remain so. The Empedokles who spoke or wrote the extant fragments is an historical, or metahistorical, fiction, authored by the first Empedokles but edited by everybody else, with everybody else's ambiguous and changeable intentions. Few of these ex officio editors are or have been interested in dealing with the text on its own terms. This accidental fiction, the author of the fragments, is the only Empedokles we have. The one thing we know about him now may not always been true: he is the author of some excellent short poems.

"The original form of a philosophy," Eliot claims, "cannot be poetic." This statement seems to me not only wrong; it seems to me quite close to a precise inversion of the truth. Yet Eliot is firm in his position. "Without a doubt," he says,

the effort of the philosopher proper, the man who is trying to deal with ideas in themselves, and the effort of the poet, who may be trying to realize ideas, cannot be carried on at the same time.[5]

I have a hunch that most pronouncements poets make about the ultimate nature of poetry are actually quite personal revelations about the particular kinds of poetry they have been writing or preparing themselves to write. This is no exception to that rule – but in this case the pronouncement is revealing of the author's deeply personal involvement with philosophy as well. Eliot wrote these sentences in 1920, four years after publishing *Prufrock and Other Observations,* his first collection of poems, and three years after choosing to abandon his effectively completed dissertation on Francis Herbert Bradley's epistemology.

Eliot's decision to identify philosophy with abstract thought and poetry with feeling, and his insistence that they cannot form one enterprise, are perfectly in tune with Bradley's neo-Hegelian teaching. So indeed is his personal decision to abandon abstract for more synaesthetic thinking (or "philosophy" for "poetry"). The abandonment of philosophy is what Bradley the philosopher recommended.

Empedokles, Parmenides and other Presocratics were not bound by Eliot's straitjacket. Neither are we. We are, or can be, just as free as they to practise poetry, philosophy and science that will stand in the strong light of one another. We are also, like the Presocratics, free to seek the common root of poetry, philosophy and science, and to honor it as best we can in any kind of language that we choose. This could be verse; it could be prose; it could be both; and it could very well be neither.

The moment we leave the conceptual jail where philosophy and poetry are confined to separate cells, we find ourselves in plenty of good company as well as fresher air. We are free to walk with Lǎo Zi and with Zhuang Zi, Empedokles, Parmenides and Sophocles, Dōgen and Xuědòu. We are also free to walk with Nietzsche and with Wittgenstein, Erigena and Pascal – and with many Native

American thinkers who may never use any of these terms but in whose practice it is clear that myth is the essential mode of poetry, the essential mode of philosophy, and the link between the two. (The Haida poet Skaay is one especially fine example.)

Once outside that prison, we are also free to turn and find the poetry that exists, not on the surface but deep in the roots of the works of Aristotle, Descartes, Kant and others in the ever-narrowing funnel of the European tradition. That poetry is real enough, though rarified and frequently expressed in the very soberest of prose.

There are unionists and separatists, it seems, arguing their views in every century and country. Giordano Bruno, for example, in the last days of the Renaissance, is sure that *uera philosophia musica seu poesis et pictura est, uera pictura et est musica et philosophia, uera poesis seu musica est diuina sophia quaedam et pictura.*[6] In other words:

True philosophy is also music, poetry and painting; true painting, too, is music and philosophy; true poetry or music is a form of holy wisdom; so is painting.

Two centuries later another Neapolitan, Giambattista Vico, took a very different view – and stated his case with all the typographic theatricality of capitals, italics and contractions then at his disposal:

Che la Ragion Poetica *determina, esser'* impossibil cosa, *ch'alcuno sia e* Poeta, *e* Metafisico *equalmente* sublime: *perchè la Metafisica* astrae la mente da' sensi; *la Facoltà Poetica dev'* immergere tutta la mente ne' sensi: *la Metafisica s'innalza sopra agli* universali; *la Facoltà Poetica deve profondarsi dentro i* particolari.[7]

Leaving aside the many rhetorical changes of case and font, this is to say:

The logic of poetry renders it impossible for anyone to be equally sublime as a poet and metaphysician. This is because metaphysics abstracts the mind from the senses, while the poetic faculty necessarily plunges the entire mind into the senses. Metaphysics elevates itself to universals; the poetic faculty has to immerse itself in particulars.

I don't especially want to argue that Empedokles is "sublime." I do however want to say that there are many ways of doing metaphysics (and, of course, epistemology and ethics), just as there are many modes of poetry. The realms in which philosophy and poetry coincide seem to me far more than incidental overlaps.

Empedokles is, to be sure, less elegant than Donne, who says for instance of his friend Elizabeth Drury that

> *her pure and eloquent blood*
> *Spoke in her cheek, and so distinctly wrought*
> *That one might almost say her body thought....*

Empedokles is less elegant; less "sublime," if you like; but not in all senses less a poet – and only a little less a philosopher – for that.

The Trashing of Doctor Empedokles · 93

LEADS & SOURCES

1 These statements appear in the first of Eliot's published essays on Dante: the one he wrote he 1920 and placed at the end of *The Sacred Wood* (2nd ed., London: Methuen, 1928: 160). His later thinking on the subject is reflected in a lecture given in 1955, "Goethe as the Sage," published in *On Poetry and Poets* (London: Faber, 1957: 207–227).

2 *Providencia de Diós* (c. 1641), in *Obras completas,* ed. Felicidad Buendía, Madrid: Aguilar, 1961, vol 1: 1422.

3 "The Metaphysical Poets," in *Selected Essays* (3rd ed., London: Faber, 1951: 286).

4 "The Metaphysical Poets," 288f.

5 This again is from the early essay on Dante (*The Sacred Wood,* 162).

6 This sentence comes near the end of the first book of *De Imaginum, signorum et idearum compositione* (Frankfurt, 1591).

7 *Prinicipi di scienza nuova* (3rd ed., Napoli: Muziana, 1744), vol 2: 395.

Tim Lilburn

Philosophical Apokatastasis: On Writing and Return

WE AREN'T FROM WHERE WE ARE; we, descendents of European settlers, don't come from this ground. We have our graves here; we have spent a few generations changing the land, but we've yet to take out chthonic Western Canadian citizenship. Some tasks are generational, and this one is so freshly started most of us aren't even aware we've begun it, the work of making a home where we are.

Landscapes have long, exacting apprenticeships and in the aspen country of north central Saskatchewan and in the grass land south of it Cree, Assiniboine, Lakota, Saulteux and others have finished theirs; it makes good sense to listen to what they've learned about making a home with northern prairie. But we shouldn't go further now than just a little listening; a person can't simply inhabit the fine ear of another culture through mere intention; to attempt this is to be homeless with recklessness and to risk infecting the destination culture with one's own desperate rootlessness, making it in some way a tourist site, enervating it with casual romantic traffic – and besides the fit is always poor. We've got to find our own way of being where we are, something in our past that will show us a path to our idiosyncratic way of residency, a route back for us, an *apokatastasis*. There is, of course, much that seems disastrous, place-erasing in this past – an arrogant, anthropocentric Christian ontology, a Baconian, privateering union of experimental science, technology and human enrichment. But it's from our past, some part of it, that we have to come: this, after all, is domicile as well.

I suspect that the way to where we are is through plain desire – and on this, on eros, its poverty, its leaping, the Western intellectual tradition has much to say that is surprisingly acute. What I want to do is speak again a few of the foundational works of Western erotics – here the *Phaedrus*, Plato's dialogue on love and the soul – in the hope that probing, not-wholly-comprehending restatement will nudge me closer to what seems necessary, yet seemingly unenterable: the erotic life. Such a life, even the roaming of its faintest edges, I sense, is all I have to bring me home. This re-saying of books will be a re-enactment of the flow of experience that they parse and will bring a small interior correction. The fact that these books can be read in this way sets them apart from almost all contemporary ones. What follows is not exegesis but apothegmata, especially of Socrates, his interlocutors and of Odysseus, the one he remembers and re-imagines as model. We become what we attend to. Perhaps the book will be an animal coming toward us out of the forest. So, the *Phaedrus*. But first we must pass through a ghost. The shape of Odysseus floats in this work, haunting, as it does in others. So, first Odysseus, the sleepy one, the one who relentlessly sleeps.

⁋ That one: resourceful, rash, from whom no trick is hidden (*Iliad* XXIII:730), the many-minded man, the man of many turns, that one, watery, acrobatically-witted, drowsy, skillful, much-contriving, flight-headed Odysseus, who must stay seven years in a cave on an island "where the navel of the sea is": here he comes to weep for home: none, swears Menelaos, swears Antiklea (*Odyssey* XI:216), have touched the exemplary affliction of this one, none suffered like Odysseus. Calypso, his guard, celestial lover, sole permanent inhabitant of omphalic Ogygia, Odysseus' guide, is the daughter of Atlas, whose knowledge of the underworld ("the depths of the whole sea") is pre-eminent, Atlas who is the guardian of the tree-like way between heaven and earth. His love-eager daughter promises to conceal nothing from her weeping, unwilling man, the drowsy one, the sleepy one, the versatile-minded wretch insatiate in tales: she shows him how to build the ship that will take him to within sight of the island of a people who are equal to the gods, through whom the gods ventriloquize their hidden minds (VI:12), the Phaiaikians who eventually deliver the thought-lit man home. She gives him the adze and the double-bladed ax, occult tools, to build this ship; she takes him to the part of her island where alder, poplar, fir muscle, inch to the heavens: by means of the heaven-entering trees he will make his way. She is his psychopomp, overseeing Odysseus' purification, his instruction, bathing and clothing him in preparation for his journey, teaching him that he must accomplish all that he must do now alone, without "escort of gods." Other guides are the daimonic Phaiaikians themselves, famous as eros-like intermediaries: they offer the man of rapid thoughts their own thought-steered ships, "as swift as any wing or thought," vehicles of ecstasy, as a means of going back, and lay him down in a leveling trance on the shores of Ithaka, exquisite goods from their perfect home stacked around him.

Odysseus' travels both before and after his incubation in the cave of Calypso – a place of beauty and poverty, surrounded by blooming vines, surrounded by fields of violet and wild parsley, the source of four rivers, a place where the birds sleep, near which Odysseus groans and pounds his heart with tears (v:83), locus of ravishment and compunction, a school of fundamental desire – his travels to and from this hidden, infiltrating place are unlike ordinary voyages; like the hero Lemminkäinen in the Finnish folk epic *Kalevala* – the "handsome man with the far-roving mind" (*Kalevala* 26:31), the "reckless" one, the "rascal" – Odysseus' is an enchanted form of travel, filled with unrealism, including an underworld descent. He leaves Troy and sacks Ismarus, city of the Kikones, Thracian allies of the Trojans: up to this point, his adventures, though heroic, are not outsized; yet as he rounds Malea, carrying a goat skin bag of black, sweet wine, one part mixed with twenty parts water, given him by Maron, priest of Apollo, who lives in the tree-thick grove of Phoebus Apollo, he's driven off course (ix:80–1), and suddenly what happens to him takes on the enormity of vision or nightmare. Giants, monsters, mammothly implausible acts – everything inflated, grotesque, the hyperbole of an unguarded psyche, shimmering with the exaggeration of ekstasis. Like the author-hero in the poem of Parmenides, like the sea-going servant hero in John Skaay's Haida long poem *The One They Hand Along,* Odysseus travels within now along the axis mundi, through a thick cosmic world of farouche striving.

Odysseus' numinous adventures after rounding Malea have several shamanic features, as has often been noted.* There is his ambivalent celestial marriage to Calypso, helping to launch his travels; there is the black wine of

Maron, the "godly drink," known to few, resembling trance-inducing mushrooms and tobacco juice Eliade says Ugrian and Jivaro shamans took. Maron lives in the grove of Apollo in northern Greece, home place of Hyperborean Apollo; this double association with the god points unmistakably to an ecstatic calling: Aristeas of Proconnesus, a famous seer mentioned by Herodotus, a northerner as well, fell into a trance in which his soul was "seized" by Apollo; after this, he was capable of bilocation, his soul tumbling from him as a raven as he accompanied the god. Abaris, also a northerner, also with powers to end pestilences and quell earthquakes, carried a golden arrow, this standing for his link with Apollo and his capacity for magical flight. Odysseus' seclusion in the cave on Ogygia, further, replicates the immurement of the ecstatic candidate in the bush – Odysseus' "bush" is not only Calypso's cave but also the wilderness of the sea – during which his fellow villagers supposed him dead, devoured by monsters, devoured by a god, so that when he returned he was not recognized but thought to be a ghost, just as Penelope supposes Odysseus dead and cannot see him as her husband when he speaks to her in their home. Odysseus' sleepiness, his "relentless sleep" (xii:372) on several occasions throughout his journey is the lethargic drowsiness of ecstatic candidacy, prelude to the leaving of the visible world in transfixity; Chukchee shamans achieved their flight to the center of the world, to the underworld, then into the celestial realms, during such states in the "canoe" of the drum, their state called a "sinking": the man of rapid thoughts, sleepy Odysseus accomplishes his transit to Hades "in a black ship" and returns to Ithaka in thick slumber in a mind-driven craft. Odysseus' remarkable suffering, his god-fashioned disquiet, is the initiatory sickness or anxiety central to the shaping of ecstatics throughout northeast Asia.

The tree, poplar, birch, willow, appears throughout the *Odyssey*; it is the same tree that in Siberian ceremonialism is the means by which a person moves along the axis mundi; it is the cosmic tree itself, offering entry to the world of the dead and the heavenly sectors. Odysseus enters Hades, following Circe's instruction, through the poplar groves of Persephone, near which, a short way on, is the "moldy hall" of the underworld (x:509–12); he arrives at the island of the god-equal Phaiaikians in a craft worked from Calypso's heaven-nudging grove; he draws himself from the gravitational field of the Sirens, insuring the continuation of his ecstatic undertaking, by having himself tied to the tall mast of his ship. The pattern and purpose of Odysseus' journey also has ecstatic marks: a descent to the dead, effecting a restoration of political equilibrium, the original conditions of home. Like all mythic, interior travel, Odysseus' adventures reach to reestablish communication between earth and heaven, the ecstatic task – he comes to acquiesce to the gods – which in turn achieves the removal of social corruption; it is a political as well as a personal purification.

But Odysseus is more than shamanic: he is the advance scout of something newer, the possessor of a cluster of qualities that Socrates in the *Phaedrus* will associate with the practice of philosophy. In fact Odysseus is a philosophical exemplar in his solitary apartness, his large capacity for travel to extreme places both within himself and the noumenal regions, in his burgeoning passivity to divine exigence, in his stripping, in his daimonic affliction, but above all in his affective apokatastatic nostalgia; the one thing he does not lose in the course of his unparalleled suffering is his longing for home: it is to just this form of singleheartedness that he is stripped.

⸨ So first the historia of the dialogue, then its underlay of theoria, its bright hiddenness.

Socrates meets Phaedrus, the youngish man for whom the work is named, just as Phaedrus is about to leave the city for a walk outside the walls, where he hopes, in country silence, to learn by heart a talk given earlier that day to a small group of friends by Lysias, his beloved, on the preferability of the non-lover as a sexual partner. Phaedrus has appeared elsewhere in Plato, in the *Symposium,* where he was the "father" of the speeches, instigating the praises of eros with the complaint that too little reverence was shown the god (*Symposium* §177c). In his own encomium there, he exposed himself as a romantic sentimentalist: love is a great god, of immeasurable benefit to humankind, of special benefit to beloved youths. Here we find him amatively leagued with the sophist Lysias, a glittering, hugely celebrated author; and while Phaedrus remains credulous, we discover he has shifted his loyalties from one idealism to another: it is now the luminous efficiency, the sweet, pillaging muscle of charm in seduction that he esteems. He is staggered by the virtuosity of the speech given by his beloved hours before – a copy of it bulges priapically beneath his tunic – its audacious trickery, purportedly usable by anyone, aimed at the importuning of a beautiful boy by someone who is not in love with him: the fact that the speech apparently has nothing to do with any conviction on the part of the one who made it simply adds to its dazzle, makes it seem even more breath-takingly masterful: Lysias has produced it as nothing more than a lit advertisement for his flashing rhetorical facility, yet Phaedrus is moved by the elegance and cleverness of these remarks as if they were actually beautiful – he responds to the glitter of Lysias' intelligence with Corybantic zeal (*Phaedrus* 228b); as with love, the ersatz seems genuine to him; he's moved, he's moved. He greets Socrates with a further shiver of delight: here's the perfect companion with whom to rehearse what he's heard this morning, since, he says, Lysias, "in a round about way," is interested in love, as Socrates is known by all to be. Socrates agrees with the suggestion that he join him in a walk in the country and that he serve as an audience for Phaedrus' recitation of Lysias' speech; he repeatedly asks Phaedrus to lead him as they move away from the city; he seems helpless in his desire to hear what Phaedrus has heard; but as they begin their stroll, it is Socrates who suggests that they "leave the path" and go down to the Ilisus. The two are on a dialectical journey as soon as they leave the usual way and go down to the water, an interior ranging.

The banks of the Ilisus, we soon see, are alive with psychagogic import: a plane tree, sacred to Dionysus, god of wine and mystic ecstasy, stands near the water; from beneath it, the water appears to flow. The scene pulls into memory Calypso's cave, that place of erotic instruction, school of sorrow and remembering, the grove in which it is set, the source of four rivers (*Odyssey* v:57–73), but also many other depictions from the ancient world of the Tree of Life with the Water of Life flowing either beneath it or from it. The presence of the tree sacred to Dionysus, maker of a descent to the underworld to rescue his mother and an ascent to heaven, recalls the shamanic labours of Odysseus.

Both Phaedrus and Socrates remark on the oddness of

the place in Socrates' experience: he *never* travels outside the city walls; landscape and trees, Socrates declares himself, hold no interest for him (230c–d); he requires, it seems, Phaedrus' leading or that of another guide (230d) to move at all in this peculiar, alien terrain. But, unexpectedly, it is the urban, humanistic Socrates who is most affected by the scene they have come upon, talking excitedly at length about the beauty of the tree, the river, the grassy bank; Phaedrus is startled by this strange effulgence. Further, it is Socrates who identifies correctly the mythical significance of the spot: it is near the place where Boreas, the god of the north wind, kidnapped Orithyia, daughter of Erektheus, king of Athens. Socrates corrects Phaedrus, his supposed guide, faux psychopomp, who had assumed that the kidnapping had occurred precisely where they stood, not, as it did, two or three hundred yards downstream. Boreas lived in Thrace – Dionysus as well had associations with Thrace, the shamanic location – and had taken the king's daughter there, chthonic nature swallowing the city, where she gave birth to twin boys, both winged like birds. Boreas is known to have lived also in the shape of a horse and sired by the mares of Erikhthonios twelve colts so soft of hoof that they did not bend the heads of the wheat as they smoothed over a field or cause a ripple on the water if they flashed on the sea. All Borean associations with the place suggest the power of magical flight. An altar, Socrates tells Phaedrus, has been erected to the god of the wind, elemental force – in human form, he is always bearded, muscular – downstream where a walker would cross to pass into Agra (229c). Socrates later will speak of horses himself in religious ascent; horses, as well as ecstatic ships, as well as birds, were instrumental throughout the ceremonial religions of northern Asia, throughout aboriginal North America, enabling the travel of ekstasis. Socrates, though out of place, is peculiarly intimate with the significance and beauty of the river, the tree, the slope: in such surroundings, with their suggestions of Dionysiac passion and transcendence, however, Lysias' speech, unmodified by the city, is reconfigured and its shabbiness, when Phaedrus gets around to reading it, shows with embarrassing clarity. In love matters, in matters of Dionysiac intensity, in the comprehending of the daimonic import of things in nature, the apparently bumbling Socrates, sleepy, pliant, proves to be surprisingly adept.

¶ Yet Socrates, autochthonic, one who knows, declares himself to be unseated by Phaedrus' recitation of Lysias' slim speech: what puts him in ecstasy (234d), though, is not what Lysias says or how he says it but the effect of Lysias' words on his lover who is radiantly moved as he reads what his beloved has composed. Socrates is arrested by Phaedrus' permeability, the way the speech of another has placed a "Bacchic frenzy" in him; he is caught by Phaedrus' erotically intent passivity – this, after all, is his own philosophical stance, part of the "ten thousandfold poverty" his "devotion to the god" has brought him (*Apology* 23c). Phaedrus thinks Socrates is joking when he lauds his delight; this is the second time Phaedrus doubts the seriousness of Socrates: the first time was when Socrates had been beside himself in praise of the Dionysiac scene they had entered, the bank slope, the river, the tree. Phaedrus does not think well about matters of emotional intensity: oddly, he does not recognize the category of things which includes the frenzy his beloved's speech has placed in him. Though he undergoes it, he does not note it or esteem it: it is not surprising, then, that he fails to cultivate it.

Socrates' own permeability, the substance of his philosophy, rests, in part, on his conviction of his ignorance – the one thing, aside from "erotic matters," about which he claims any knowledge (*Apology* 21d; *Phaedrus* 235c) – his emptiness, positionlessness; Socrates carries no speeches beneath his clothes. His insistence upon his ignorance here (235d), his insistence, a little later, on his incompetence (236d), is not ironic but is an assertion of his philosophical poetics: none of his ideas are his own; he assembles no system; he is "an empty jar," the words of others streaming through his ears (235d). But Socrates' reachability, his affective availability to the speech of others, is unlike Phaedrus': it is modified by *phronesis*; through all that presses on him, he puts his hand toward the one thing that corrects desire, something *seen,* something ravishing, that holds in memory, that alters what comes after it; he has not lost his wits as a lover (236a) as Phaedrus has; he has discernment. His self-awareness also means that he recognizes the frenzy his permeability places in him as a treasureable thing and he grooms it – later we will see how this grooming involves attachment to a particular form of memory.

His response to Lysias' remarks is lukewarm – the rhetorician, he says, just has "spoken in a clear and concise manner, with a precise turn of phrase," though, Socrates complains, he has repeated himself as if he had no real interest in his topic. The appraisal naturally staggers the enraptured Phaedrus. Socrates, with some clumsiness, goes further: he has no doubt that he can make not only a different speech – his breast is full, after all; he is not without interest (235c) – but a better one. He immediately regrets this boast, though, as Phaedrus presses him to give such a speech and sets conditions upon it – what Socrates says must contain more and better points without repeating any of Lysias' observations except the one that claims that the lover is mad while the non-lover is not. It's impossible, Socrates protests, for him not to appear a ridiculous dilettante before the gleaming professionalism of Lysias. Phaedrus threatens to deprive Socrates of all reports of speeches in the future if he doesn't go ahead and make a competing speech, and Socrates, a "lover of speeches," feels his arm bent toward making some remarks of his own on the destructive madness of love, but he sets his own condition: he will cover his head as he speaks. Odysseus covered his head with his purple mantle in the court of Alkinoos out of shame for the tears he shed listening to Demodokos' account of events at Troy (*Odyssey* VIII:84–6). The shame that Socrates feels here is less for his words than for their effect on the impressionable Phaedrus: he cannot bring himself to read their monstrous effect on his interlocutor's unguarded face. Unlike Socrates, Phaedrus is not aware of his permeability; he doesn't make his wits qualify it; he doesn't profess it, practice it, as Socrates does: in his sentimentality, he is its victim.

Socrates' first speech, a head-covered speech, roughly traces Lysias': Phaedrus cannot imagine any other sort of speech on love (235b); Socrates, artful, correct psychagogue, carefully does not exceed his anticipations. Since the purpose of Lysias' talk is the duping of a young man into granting sexual favours to an older man with no emotional ties to him, it works hard to undermine the position of the lover. The lover is contemptible, mad, ill, says Lysias; the lover is an amorous calculator, "keeping his eye on the balance sheet," giving the boy no more than a fair return for his acceding to sexual requests. The lover is naturally boastful – everyone will hear of his success with the boy – and he is untrustworthy in the long run as well: he inevitably will move on from his present beloved; his insecurity, further, makes him crafty: he will starve the beloved of the friendships of the wealthy and intelligent, keeping him pathetically dependent. Everyone should feel sorry for lovers, Lysias urges, not admire them. Nonlovers, on the other hand, are disinterested, magnanimous, generous, because they are not crazed, made possessive or irritably protective of their own dignity by love; they do not "follow us, knock on our door," embarrassing the wanted beauty with their ridiculous importunacy. Love, says Lysias, is a disease so virulent that those who suffer it once lose all resistance to any new onslaught. Even the lover himself is aware that he is sick: he helplessly regards his inability to get himself under control; fully appreciating his chaotic state, he refuses to accept responsibility for decisions he made while in it.

Socrates heaves Lysias' strategic subversion of the lover over the top, writing the figure large as he does the "feverish city" in the *Republic* for Glaucon, that young man with slightly sinister political enthusiasms, who, like Phaedrus, has insufficient prudence to read the soul – and once more the point of the distortion is to repel, nudging an interlocutor from a jammed erotic state. The lover, he says, has utterly lost his mind, is everything Lysias says he is, deceitful, irritable, as well as being "absolutely devastating to the cultivation" of the beloved's soul (241c); imperious, he works out of a mad insecurity to make the young man weaker and inferior to himself; the lover, older, is also physically disgusting, with parts that are "a misery even to hear ... mentioned, let alone actually handle...." But Socrates unexpectedly stops when Phaedrus assumes he is only half way through: he has yet to praise the non-lover. He has, however, presented a lurid version of Lysias' lover – one so grotesquely drawn it might undermine even the tenability of the position of the non-lover – from which a supporter of the Lysianic position could be expected to recoil: he has given Phaedrus grounds to regret his enthusiasm. He halts because, he says, he has heard "a voice coming from this very spot," (242c) the noumenal river bank with its associations with chthonic gods, his daimonion, the divine voice that always turns him away from whatever "incorrect" thing he is about to do (*Apology* 31d, 40a). He says he sees now he has been impious in his denigration of love, which is actually, he now understands, "a god or something divine," and having said what he did is in need of purification, the famous purification of Stesichorus, a palinode, a recantatory poem erasing what was said before.

Phaedrus misses much of this. He believes Socrates' speech to be an incomplete copy of Lysias' – he has conflated the two individuals from the beginning of the dialogue; he fails to see Socrates' remarks as caricature; he does not recoil from their exaggeration – and so for him Socrates' shame has a pedagogical significance: Socrates models for his interlocutor a way out of his infatuation with Lysias' glittering performance, his elegant simulacrum of insight; but Phaedrus is not reached by this piece of Socratic instruction: the nature of his permeability makes him ravishable, but not educable.

❡ Socrates' reversal, his purification, is initially, surprisingly, a defence of madness. Certain forms of insanity, he says, are wanted, the words, we can imagine, rising in the intense listening of the erotic, the philosophical, individual. The beneficial insanities are mantic, engined by the god, driving one away from the lesser good of self-control (244d): they cause one to leave the path (229a); they drive one off course (*Odyssey* IX:80–1), making those so afflicted out-of-place, disturbed (*Phaedrus* 249a), estranged in the Socratic manner (*Theaetetus* 149a): such a self-displaced, stirred craning, at its furthest reach, is the state of philosophy (*Phaedrus* 249c–d), an alacrity, an erotic reachability not wholly unlike Phaedrus' delight, but pulled by an object that does not contort it to the disadvantage of an individual – a telos the pursuit of which unexpectedly unfolds the person into the musicality of virtue.

There is the madness of the oracle, says Socrates – the prophetess at Delphi, the priestesses at Dodona (244b) – who are "out of their minds when they perform that fine work of theirs for all of Greece"; there is the therapeutic madness, the sharp psychagogic, diagnostic inspiration, that discerns the individual in need of rites and purifications, lifting from them the guilt of ancient crimes (244d–e). There is the Bacchic frenzy the Muses place in particular poets, which drives their work past that of writers with mere technical mastery. A demonstration of such a superseding by one who has been driven out of his mind (245a) appears presently in the dialogue: Socrates, in the palinode, is Muse-goaded; Lysias is never anything other than clever.

Socrates then interrupts his taxonomy of benign, "god-sent" madness to give an account of what the soul is like, but admits that he can get no closer than an image to the actuality of the soul, since to say what the soul truly is would require, he claims, not only an exceedingly long account, but is a task only a god could manage (246a). The soul, he says, his lucid image of interiority apparently gusted into him, is like the union of a charioteer and a team of horses, both of which are winged, like the mind of Odysseus, like the offspring of Boreas and Orithymia: one of the horses is beautiful and good, while the other "has the opposite sort of bloodline." The wings of the soul – all of the soul is winged – are what is most divine about it and, thus, divine things – wisdom, beauty, goodness – cause them to strengthen; foul, ugly things atrophy them.

The winged human soul, at some early point, joins the procession of gods, led by Zeus, whom the other eleven deities follow without question: the procession moves through heaven "looking after everything" (246e), each god accomplishing a particular cosmological task: anyone who wishes may follow them – there is no jealousy among those who are divine. They begin their ascent to the banquet at the rim of heaven, and the gods' chariots move easily to that place – they have exquisite balance, are compactly under control – but human souls who follow them have difficulty, the bad horse, heavier, unruly, pulling the chariot back to earth. What is visible from the rim of heaven is beyond description, yet it speaks directly, nourishingly, to intelligence, offering it intuitively certain, non-reportable views of justice, interior order, knowledge – contemplative clarities "of what really is what it is."

The soul that "follows the god most closely, making itself most like the god" (248a), gets at best only a partial view of the colourless, shapeless, intellectible things beyond heaven's rim: the head of the charioteer, struggling with his horses, rises a little "up to the place outside" and sees what lies beyond for a moment, then is pushed aside and down again as other chariots weave and tangle and fight to the rim (248a–b): if its partial view of what is true is insufficient, it loses its wings entirely and falls frighteningly back to earth. The soul's wings may be regrown, but this involves the lucky, relentless work of a number of lifetimes and requires that a soul consecutively choose the life of a philosopher, or, what is virtually the same but somewhat less unlikely, a lover of beauty or a person tending toward erotic love.

A philosopher's mind grows wings because in memory it keeps close to what it has seen: like Odysseus, the philosopher does not fail to recall the quintessential nourishment of his original state. One does this by maintaining an alert receptivity to those reminders of the unparalleled, extra-celestial things, such as the beauty of a boy. Eccentricities flourish in this remembering; people think the person so recollected is "disturbed and rebuke him for this"; the divine possession is invisible to all. Such recollections cause one to be cast out of one's life, mantically alacritous: one then is caught up in the fourth, the paramount, the sublating, madness, which is philosophy: the pre-eminent moment in this frenzy, this particular ekstasis, is the appearance, through memory, of apokatastatic desire.

⁋ So Socrates and Phaedrus sit on the river bank in the afternoon heat, talking: daimonic kidnappings, flying chariots, interior wings, pre-natal visions.

Odysseus achieves his passage to heaven-like Phaiakia by way of trees cut from Calypso's grove, assembled into a boat under her instruction; the Altaic shaman enters the celestial home of Bai Ülgän carried by the soul of a light-coloured horse which has been sacrificed in front of his specially erected yurt, its spine broken after a birch branch has been passed over its back, no blood being allowed to touch the ground or the sacrificer during this ceremony. The traveler in the Socratic palinode moves to a point beyond the rim of heaven in a chariot pulled by one good horse and one bad horse, physical forms, it is usually thought, for the contesting powers of reason and passion. For all three, the ascent is accomplished with sexual emotion – Odysseus desires a return to Penelope; the philosopher's ascent begins when an apokatastatic nostalgia is quickened in him by the repeated sight of a beautiful young man; the ecstatic travel of a Siberian shaman is powered by his erotic love for his *ayami* or tutelary spirit.

The palinode has no ontological significance: it sets in place no dogmas about the nature of the soul or its life before birth; it makes no theological claims; it has nothing to say about the physical structure of the universe. The Socratic account of winged ascent is nothing more than a heavily wrought, action-filled image meant to render the soul (246a) for an interlocutor who loves speeches but has demonstrated an incompetence in the reading of souls. It is also a heuristic, effacing itself immediately as hypothesis, intended to do nothing more than to lure and shape desire, which evokes nothing other than the full range of desire's secret, almost unspeakable imagination, which the desirer, if he experiences it at all, experiences it strangely as nostalgia: full erotic reach appears as remembering. The beauty of the boy is not the only source of anamnesis: a heuristic tale like the ascent account in the palinode works just as well. Phaedrus repeatedly sees resemblances of the surpassing things – he is quite attracted to such things, speeches, beautiful, young males – but he does not remember because his senses do not discern adequately what is before them (249e): he cannot see moral beauty, of course, justice, moderation, but also he cannot fathom physical beauty or literary resonance. Neither takes him anywhere; neither quickens in him the eros which is philosophy.

⁋ So Phaedrus and Socrates sit on the river bank in the heat of the afternoon, talking, talking. The day is hot; the stream is cool.

Beauty is one of the radiant things the soul saw as its head momentarily lifted above the high rim before it was yanked downward by the team it could never control, that had never stopped pulling, before it was shouldered aside by other swept-away souls wild to see "that blessed and spectacular vision" in the hectic, noisy moment of rapturous insight: feathers broke off in the mêlée and forgetting immediately began. Other things were visible in that roiling moment – justice as it is, wisdom as it is – but they receded further with the soul's descent into the body, so that now the only way to "follow the god's pattern" and return to what feeds the soul is through erotic love. The only way to do philosophy is through erotic love, philosophy as an interior availability to something that seems to be nostalgia and from which gathers a desire to re-experience the purity of what appears to be ultimate vision – thus the philosophical need of the bad horse: *all* of the soul is winged. Philosophy can be done only under these conditions because vision, says Socrates, is the least decayed of the senses; beauty, as a result, is the only one of the ultimate things that still comes through to human beings. When it is manifest to a "recent initiate" in the form of a beautiful boy, the person is flattened by an erotic wind, pain, joy; what he feels is the residue of his recent heavenly ravishing; it is a longing for the past (250d), which he construes as a love for an individual. The soul, with some trauma, returns to its feathered state. One becomes mantically singleminded – propriety is forgotten, one's friends, family, one's affairs are forgotten – thinned to one wanting. But pursuit is not all: the lover is impelled to secure an initiation for the beloved: his love madness must be transferred to the beloved and such a transferral is impossible if the beloved is not romantically captured (253c). Philosophy, certainly, is the erotic reach for the boy, but it is also the boy's reception of the lover's maieutical good will; this communicates into him what the lover knows: displacement from his life, a sort of affliction, a leaving the path, which marks the beginning of a long apprenticeship in emulating the god.

¶ In the discussion of rhetoric that takes up the last third of the dialogue, the old issue of the difference between Phaedrusian and Socratic permeability is revisited. Phaedrus, a good Lysianic, rests lightly on his loyalties: his admiration for Socrates' palinode nudges him to turn on his beloved, reporting a recent conversation with a politician in which Lysias was attacked as a mere "speech writer." Socrates objects to the condemnation: it's not writing itself that is shameful – one *could* write well, he claims – but speaking or writing shamefully or badly. But then what distinguishes good writing from bad, he wonders. This question goes to the heart of Phaedrus' character; he is enamoured of books, of writers – all writers are good, all books impressive. He admires Lysias' lack of roots, lack of place; his being a writer brings him this: the cleverness of Phaedrus' beloved means he never locates himself in a view; the writtenness of his speech means that what it says is portable, usable by anyone under almost any set of circumstances. Because he isn't embodied, nothing limits Lysias' audacity – his shocking charm, his noble wilfulness – making him, in his caprice, appear *atopos* – shiningly unlike – and godlike.

Socrates warns Phaedrus that as they try to answer the question of quality in writing, they must be careful to pass by the Siren-like influence of the cicadas who overhear them. The cicadas, sounding in the trees throughout the afternoon above the two speakers on the river bank, were once human beings themselves, who when they first heard the Muses sing were overwhelmed by the pleasure of the experience, forgetting to eat and drink in their rapt delight; they died in this state without even realizing they had done so.

Part of their role now is to report to the Muses human beings who are devoted to the arts and give to these persons "the gift from the gods they are able to give" (259b), that is, they can make those they report dearer to the Muses by making their devotion known. The cicadas themselves are not particularly dear to the divine singers – they are granted the doubtful gift of being able to indulge their monomaniacal listening without interruption for eating and drinking – nor are they devoted: they perform no art. Being seduced by a thing is not honouring it: such immolation is a form of willful self-absorption, not devotion, not honouring. The virtuosity of the cicadas is just vocal; they don't actually say anything; they are Lysianic; not only are they not dear to the Muses, they do not profoundly hear them; not hearing, they are not spoken through. Because they have been seduced, they can't bring a listener to any depth; they can charm but they can't bring one to divine places. They have greed but no madness. Phaedrus is cicada-like; he immolates himself before authorship and the fetishized artifact of the book, disappearing in his own ravishment; he is caught by the romance of the book and the romantic placelessness of the author: he carries a book under his cloak next to his skin. The charm of authorship not only immobilizes him; it keeps him on the surface of writing. He esteems the mere power of being able to move someone, to exploit a basic permeability in a listener, the muscle of the sophist, seeing this as the height of achievement and not simply the "preliminary" of philosophical maieutics (269b–c) – such is the primitivism of Phaedrus' own erotic availability.

Socrates, on the other hand, *is* dear to the Muses: he serves Calliope, muse of epic poetry, by doing philosophy (259d), that is, by replicating in his acts, his erotic craning, the ecstatic heroism recounted throughout epic literature from Sumerian poems of Inanna's descent, through the *Odyssey,* to the unnamed servant's passage to the land beneath the ocean in Skaay's *The One They Hand Along.* The one difference between the psychagoguery of Socratic rhetoric and shamanic travel is that, though both involve the direction of souls in the underworld, Socratic direction is never funereal: it draws souls, as in the Cave allegory, into some unsayable light.

❡ Good speaking and writing, Socrates says, come from one who knows the truth of his subject (260e); it is devoted to "directing souls ... not only in the law courts but also in private." Bad writing, then, simply ravishes those whose permeability is without discernment; it enchants but takes one nowhere: instead it immobilizes the soul, robbing a person of eros and its motility, its epektatic appetite, Agathon's performance in the *Symposium,* Glaucon's blueprint for the imperial city in the *Republic,* working the erotic deformities of charm's fat sleep, imperial conviciton, or dogmatism. Knowledge of the truth of one's subject comes through the dialectical practice of collection and division, where all things of the same kind – all forms of madness, say, all forms of love – are drawn together (265e), then separated into species, cut along "natural joints," the "left-handed" sort of madness being discarded, the right-handed valued. Not all can do this: only those who have undergone the anamnetic experience either through a self-quelling desire for a beautiful youth or through a speech inspiring apokatastatic nostalgia would be able to perform this dialectic: anyone unengined by such memory could be no more than self-ministering, holding in a partisan manner to whatever view of "justice" or "love" most pleased him, no play in his erotic life, conviction misconstrued consistently as understanding.

Good speech also requires a study of the nature of the soul, its various types and the effect different speeches are likely to have on various sorts of soul; such knowledge comes by means of "a long, rough path," (272c) that no one would attempt unless he had an ambition "to be able to speak and act in a way that pleases the gods as much as possible." The ability to read souls taxonomically cannot come from written accounts of rhetoric, which systematize address, shrinking the complexity of maieutics to a manual; this perpetrates the deception that lies in all writing – that the reproduction of an experience is equal to the undergoing of the experience; it does not confess the vicarious nature of writing itself. Codified, written instruction on rhetoric, like all writing that takes itself with a fatal seriousness to embody knowledge of lasting importance (277d), confuses representation, here analysis, with the thing itself (275c), imagines it identifies without remainder. Socrates has in mind works on the mechanics of rhetoric by the peers of Lysias, purporting to teach the skill of arguing what is likely – an endeavour that, even with good will, he believes to be fraudulent. It distances one from what one would know – it breeds forgetting (275a): apokatastatic remembering is an erotic enterprise and grows, at least in part, from an experience of poverty. The conditions for this poverty are erased in the identification of system with understanding: writing that takes itself as apogeal achievement truncates desire. Apodictic, exhaustive, it gives the impression that it yields clear and certain results (277d), analysis confused with authority: yet it is only the simulacrum of the term of inquiry. In fact, such writing is not even inquiry since it is no longer appetitive, epektatic. If system is taken as anything other than training or heuristic, if it is held to be a terminal state, it de-eroticizes inquiry. Phaedrus cannot imagine any exploration beyond system and its application as technique.

⁋ Odysseus arrives home because it has not left his imagination since his heart was broken during his seven years sequestering in Calypso's cave: an Odyssean stripping is the mother of erotic imagination. The lover of the youth loses himself – all sense of self-protection, all dignity – and the remembrance of home strides toward him: out of humiliation an erecting attention, out of an initiatory affliction an apokatastatic reaching. A systematic analysis of the soul that does not efface itself breeds a bogus sufficiency, inattention. But writing from someone with "a knowledge of the truth," who can defend his writing when challenged, who can make an argument that his writing is of little worth (278c–d), reminds one of one's original nature, of what one has always known but never said to oneself. Such writing can contribute to the philosophical enterprise, the quickening of an affective, apokatastatic nostalgia for an event that never occurred, the report of which draws in the whole of desire, its full stride, its unabridged imagination. The *Odyssey* and the Socratic palinode have the power to entice into being the erotic endeavour they represent – a vivifying, frightening undertaking, which will go on beyond the poem and the tale of chariots wrestling into the sky.

SOURCES

* E.A.S. Butterworth, *Some Traces of the Pre-Olympian World in Greek Literature and Myth*; E.R. Dodds, *The Greeks and the Irrational*; Zdravko Planinc, "Homeric Imagery in Plato's *Phaedrus*," in *Politics, Philosophy, Writing: Plato's Art of Caring for Souls*; Agathe Thornton, *People and Themes in Homer's Odyssey*.

Here, as elsewhere, my reading of Plato is indebted to the work of Zdravko Planinc.

Jan Zwicky

Dream Logic and the Politics of Interpretation

> I don't believe in *any* interpretation of dreams. I don't *want* to believe in dream interpretation. I will not touch this last freedom.
> – ELIAS CANETTI, *The Secret Heart of the Clock*

WE SPEAK of the interpretation of dreams, meaning by this roughly the process of rendering them intelligible. But this at once presents us with a puzzle: if we are indeed *interpreting* them, then according to one common understanding of the word, we are expounding, explicating, or rendering clear a meaning which they already possess. But why, then, do we need the interpretation? Are we not the dreamers of the dreams? Are they not efflorescences or excrescences of *our* minds? If dreams are indeed intelligible, then why do we require an interpretation to reveal this to us?

One answer: we are simply wrong in imagining dreams are products of our minds. God, or some other agent, sends them to us and constructs them according to a pattern whose logic we must always struggle to comprehend. This is a model of the epistemology and metaphysics of dreams with a long and distinguished history; but as a recent denizen of Freud's century, I prefer another course. I will begin, then, with premises that echo fundamental tenets in Freud's own theory: that dreams do indeed have meaning, and that they are the products of our own minds. I will sketch an answer to the question, "Why, then, do they require interpretation?" based on Freud's metapsychology. But I will argue that compelling as Freud's account is, it still doesn't answer the question. My thesis will be that, understood as products of a system of mental organization that Freud called 'primary process,' dreams do not, in fact, *require* interpretation in a conceptual or epistemological sense of 'require.' But the requirement nonetheless remains. I will argue that its root is political. Students of *Civilization and Its Discontents* may hear in this claim a further echo of Freud. But I will urge, against Freud, that the political requirement of an interpretation barrier between ourselves and the *logos* of primary process, while perhaps necessary for civilization as we know it, is not necessary for civilization: and that integrity, both in the wider sense, and the sense provided by Freud's metapsychological theory, requires that the wall to some extent come down. I will conclude with a sketch of one of the ways in which I take primary process – the logic of dreams – to be of interest to the pursuit of philosophy.

*

Freud's thesis that dreams are a meaningful form of human mental activity created quite a stir in Vienna when it was first aired in 1905. But it was underwritten by a yet more radical conceptual innovation, which forms the foundation of all of Freud's metapsychological work, namely the notion of *unconscious thought*.

Because, for Freud, dreams were merely one expression of a basic *form* of mental activity characteristic of a psychical system he called "the unconscious," it is to the characteristics – and paradoxes – of this system I will first turn. The question of our ability consciously to attend to and appreciate primary process thought – on which my argument about the relevance of dream-logic to philosophy must hang – is a vexed one: if it is indeed the structure of *unconscious* thought, then how, for example, can we account for the fact that we 'get' jokes – whose mechanisms, Freud argues, are those of primary process? If our appreciation is unconscious, shouldn't we be bewildered to find ourselves barking uncontrollably at an apparently nonsensical sentence? Or if, as psychoanalytically-inclined scholars like Charles Rycroft have suggested, the creative activity of many artists reveals primary process at work, how can we account for the fact that those artists appear to be quite alert and focussed while composing? It is not even clear to what extent it makes sense to call persons in a hypnotic trance 'unconscious,' when they are obviously aware of and responsive to aspects of their environment. But these are problems not so much for primary process in its alleged relation to unconsciousness, as they are for Freud's notion of the unconscious in general. By this, I do not mean to join forces with Freud's opponents, nor to suggest that there are not striking clusters of problems around attention, repression, memory, and censorship in their relation to primary process. What I do want to suggest is that these puzzles are not solved by Freud's insistence that primary process activity is unconscious and that mental activity of which we are aware always betokens its absence. On the contrary, the brilliance of Freud's notion of what he *calls* 'the unconscious' is precisely that the axes 'aware/unaware,' 'conscious/not conscious' may be the *least* helpful in establishing the crucial contrasts with "normal mental life."[1]

⸨ "Our right to assume the existence of something mental that is unconscious and to employ that assumption for the purposes of scientific work is disputed in many quarters," Freud remarks mildly near the beginning of his 1915 paper, "The Unconscious."[2] He then goes on to mount a defence which, though perhaps rhetorically overstated, is nonetheless impressive: the assumption of the existence of unconscious thought is justified because: (1) "the data of consciousness have a very large number of gaps in them; both in healthy and in sick people psychical acts often occur which can be explained only by presupposing other acts, of which, nevertheless, consciousness affords no evidence"; (2) "the assumption of there being an unconscious enables us to construct a successful procedure by which we can exert an effective influence upon the course of conscious processes"; (3) it is obvious that "at any given moment consciousness includes only a small content, so that the greater part of what we call conscious knowledge must in any case be for very considerable periods of time in a state of latency, that is to say, of being psychically unconscious"; (4) "all the categories which we employ to describe conscious mental acts, such as ideas, purposes, resolutions and so on, can be applied to [these unconscious contents]"; and finally, (5) "the existence and mode of operation of the mental unconscious" is "tangibly demonstrated" by *pre*-psychoanalytic experiments with hypnosis. Now, while these hardly constitute the "incontrovertible proof" Freud at one point claims they do, I think most people — especially in nations as heavily therapized as Canada and the USA — will grant that they constitute substantial *support* for the notion of unconscious thought. But, in the event we remain unconvinced, Freud has saved his boldest — but, I will argue, most problematic – argument for last: "in postulating [the existence of an unconscious] we are not departing a single step from our customary and generally accepted mode of thinking." That "mode," Freud claims, is manifest in our daily assumption that, on the basis of their outward behaviours, beings other than ourselves have minds. "Psychoanalysis demands nothing more," he says, "than that we should apply this process of inference to ourselves also.... If we do this, we must say: all the acts and manifestations which I notice in myself and do not know how to link up with the rest of my mental life must be judged as if they belonged to someone else: they are to be explained by a mental life *ascribed to this other person*."[3] An astonishing claim, indeed; and Freud goes on to note what is obviously wrong with it: what the argument appears to lead to is not "the disclosure of an unconscious; it leads logically to the assumption of another, second *consciousness* which is united in one's self with the consciousness one knows."[4] – And those who resist the notion of "an unconscious *psychical*" are not likely to buy the notion of an unconscious *consciousness* "of which its own possessor knows nothing."[5] Additionally, the processes that appear to characterize unconscious thought "enjoy a high degree of mutual independence, as though they had no connection with one another, and knew nothing of one another" – hence, Freud thinks, we would be logically compelled to admit the possible existence of a third, fourth, indeed an unlimited number of, consciousnesses, all of which we know nothing about – and this is absurd. Most tellingly, though, he claims that these "latent processes" have characteristics "which seem alien to us, or even incredible, and which run directly counter to the attributes of consciousness with which we are familiar."

From all of which he concludes that there cannot exist a second conscious*ness*; rather, we must "modify our inference about ourselves" and say that what is proved is "the existence of psychical acts which lack consciousness."

Here, I think it is appropriate to pause a moment in surprise: isn't the *point* of the exercise to demonstrate a whole realm of mental activity "of which its own possessor knows [almost] nothing"? And if the course of this mental activity — once, somehow, made known — strikes us as "alien," "incredible," and "run[ning] directly counter to the attributes of consciousness with which we are familiar," why *shouldn't* we conclude exactly what Freud tells us we cannot: namely, that it isn't ours? I take it that the arguments cited previously to justify the claim that unconscious mental activity exists still go through, bizarre though that activity may seem. But here another puzzle must strike us; *one* of those arguments rested on the observation that obviously not all conscious knowledge is, actually, at any given moment, conscious. Freud's rhetorical question — *Where, then, does it go?* — masks a genuine tension between this observation and what is asserted about the processes governing unconscious thought. For the force of the observation hinges on our admitting the latency of what, at other times, is conscious knowledge — our teaching schedule, our Swiss bank account number — and which we are willing to admit is *our* conscious knowledge because it *seems* like our conscious knowledge: it has all the familiar characteristics. But it is precisely this claim — that unconscious thought has the characteristics of conscious thought — that Freud denies a few pages later. What is going on? Though our intuitions about the existence and to some extent the nature of unconscious thought may remain with Freud, the argument that would focus these intuitions seems to be disintegrating into chaos.

What these quandaries point to, in good latent fashion, is that in Freud's conception, the *fundamental* distinction between what he calls 'conscious' and 'unconscious' thought is a *structural* one. There is not an 'on-off' attention-switch involved in the transition from one to the other, but something more like a change of state. Indeed, where there *is* something like an on-off switch – our latent knowledge of our teaching schedule, or Swiss bank account number – Freud will argue that the form, the pattern of the thought, must be the same as that of conscious thought. Such thought, he appears to have maintained, is nothing more than conscious thought without the gain on the amplifier turned up; *and for that reason* – that is, because of its structural similarity to 'normal' 'waking' thought, *in spite* of its overt affinity with dream-thought in being non-conscious – Freud distinguished it from 'genuinely' 'unconscious' thought by the rubric "preconscious." Jokes and parapraxes, on the other hand, are structured like dreams, he argued – *and for that reason,* and *in spite* of the fact that we are demonstrably conscious when they occur, they are to be classed as products of the unconscious. Though I do not wish to deny that we are frequently asleep when we dream, it seems to me the terminology is getting in the way of the insight. The insight is that there are two distinct *logoi* operating in human mental activity, of which we are, at different times and variously, conscious and unconscious.[6] These two *logoi* – the one informing dreams, slips of the tongue, jokes and neurotic symptoms, the other informing 'normal' waking thought – Freud called, respectively, primary and secondary process.

⁋ Freud spends a brief section of the paper "The Unconscious" outlining the characteristics of "the so-called *primary psychical process.*" This is essentially a condensed version of material treated in §E, of chapter VII of *The Interpretation of Dreams.* A rather different, but equally synoptic, treatment of the two processes is provided in the 1911 paper, "Formulations on the Two Principles of Mental Functioning." Fully to understand some of this material, and more importantly to grasp its significance for the unity of Freud's later metapsychological reflections, we would have to return to the earliest and, I believe, most startlingly original of Freud's psychological writings, the incomplete "Project for a Scientific Psychology" (drafted and abandoned in 1895). This would, however, take us too far afield. I must here confine myself to noting that it constituted Freud's attempt to provide a physically reductionist explanation of consciousness, based on his clinical observations of the clusterings of characteristics that distinguished dreams and hypnotic states from "normal mental life." The attempt at reductionism failed;[7] the clusterings continued to assert themselves. It is to Freud's characterizations of these *logoi* I now turn. Following this, we will be ready to return to the central question of this discussion: Why do dreams require interpretation?

⁋ In 1915, in §V of "The Unconscious," Freud writes:

By the process of displacement [*in the system* Ucs.] *one idea may surrender to another its whole quota of cathexis; by the process of* condensation *it may appropriate the whole cathexis of several other ideas.*[8] *I have proposed to regard these two processes as distinguishing marks of the so-called primary psychical process.*

Freud considered them 'distinguishing,' I believe, because of their importance for the "Project's" account of the ontogenetic relationship between primary and secondary process (from which relationship they in fact derive their names). There are, however, a number of other features, on the surface every bit as distinctive as condensation and displacement, that also characterize 'unconscious' thought. These include an emphasis on psychical, rather than external, reality; timelessness; a tolerance of paradox and contradiction; and the capacity to "exer[t] on somatic processes an influence of intense plastic power which the conscious act can never do." In primary process, thoughts are linked by associations "of a kind [e.g., homonyms] ... scorned by our normal thinking and relegated to the use of jokes."

Secondary process, by contrast, appears to be all that primary process is not: its operation is predicated on a fundamental distinction between self and non-self, as well as consistently observed distinctions between psychic and external reality, and among individual images and perceptions as well. It recognizes, and operates according to, linear orders in space and time, and adheres to the standard inference patterns of basic logic – in particular, it respects the principle of non-contradiction. Judgement, which doesn't occur in primary process, is its central function. Grammatical and logical language-use is its hallmark.

What, then, for Freud constitutes an interpretation of a dream? The closest to a theoretical statement I have been able to find occurs at the beginning of chapter 11 of *The Interpretation of Dreams*:

> ... *'interpreting' a dream implies assigning a 'meaning' to it – that is, replacing it by something which fits into the chain of our mental acts as a link having a validity and importance equal to the rest.*

What is this 'something'? Freud's descriptions of his practice throughout make clear that it is an account, in words, that makes explicit the associations of the various elements of the dream with all other relevant thoughts and ideas, and which then arranges these verbally-clothed renderings in a way that "makes sense" – that is, in a way that untangles the discontinuities, compressions, and contradictions produced by condensation, displacement, and the dream-work's tendency to disregard time. An interpretation, then, is a secondary process elaboration and re-structuring of material initially presented in primary process: it is, to paraphrase Wittgenstein, the substitution of an expression in one *logos* for an expression in another. The end result of this substitution or replacement is that we become able to understand what was originally presented "in a manner which is in the highest degree bewildering and [apparently] irrational." This, in interesting and obvious ways, echoes our experience of utterances in languages with which we are entirely unfamiliar. An interpretation, in short, is a translation.

Indeed, the whole point of psychotherapy in the treatment of neurotic symptoms is to provide a translation in this sense: 'the talking cure,' as one of Freud's and Breuer's earliest patients described it, aims to take the mute gestures of primary process and attach them to word-presentations in order that we may bring them to 'consciousness.' And because of the peculiarities we've noted in Freud's notion of the unconscious, it turns out that this 'bringing to consciousness' cannot amount to 'becoming *aware* of them'; it must, rather, amount to something more like coming to understand what the gestures (do, already) mean. To understand them through familiar word-presentations, according to the clinical theory, *just is* to lift repressions and to begin the process of healing. Thus Freud's remark in §vi of "The Unconscious": "a complete divergence of their trends; a total severance of the two systems, is what above all characterizes a condition of illness." The 'translations' of psychoanalysis are viewed by Freud as one way of re-establishing the link.

There are many things that might strike us as interesting and problematic by turns about this conception of interpretation as translation; I shall focus briefly on two. The first concerns the identity of the 'content' as it passes from one system to the next: if, in order to understand it, we have to alter the *structure* of the thought – change its grammar, as it were – on what grounds can we be confident that, so altered, the thought as represented in the second system *really is* the thought as it came to us in the first? Isn't what-the-thought-is in some important measure a function of the way it is expressed? It is, I believe, no accident that this puzzle is precisely paralleled by a purely literary phenomenon: the alleged 'impossibility' of translating poetry. A poem's meaning, it is often maintained by those who read or write poetry in more than one language, is inalienably tied to the language in which it is written – a good poem is dependent on every detail of its articulation – sound play within particular grammatical constructions, relationships among rhyme, rhythm, and sense, tonal effects supervenient on culturally-determined factors reflected in idiom and dialect – etc. The meaning of a good poem is a product of – or perhaps just *is* – a complex lingua-chemical equilibrium; to translate it is to change its state. How could the translated product possibly possess the same meaning as the original?

Well: this is precisely wherein lies the art of the translator. For the fact is, good – even brilliant – translations of poems do exist. And so do good – even brilliant – interpretations of dreams. How this could be so deserves more careful reflection than the subject usually receives – more careful than space here allows. I raise the issue, and draw out the analogy between interpreting dreams and translating poems, to note only that the puzzle points not to the absolute impossibility of translation between primary and secondary process, nor to the need for a reversion to 'hard core' syntax-insensitive theories of meaning; rather, because our comprehension of poetry shows that sense is, in some measure, a function of form, and because translation is still, in some measure, possible, the puzzle points to the need for further reflection on the *relation* between form-sensitive and form-insensitive conceptions of meaning. – Or perhaps to the need for a conception of meaning that manages to sidestep the perennially-vexed notions of 'form' and 'content' altogether.

The second puzzle on which I wish to focus grows directly out of the first: the one respect in which the interpretation of dreams on Freud's model *cannot* be said to resemble the translation of poetry is the absence of two *languages*. It is, we might argue, precisely the characteristic *absence* of language, primary process's refusal to adhere to basic grammatical rules, that makes translation into secondary process *necessary*. The obvious next question is: in what sense, then, is it *translation*? How can it be translation, except in a metaphorical sense, if language is involved on only one side?

The *Oxford English Dictionary* marks three main divisions in its definition of the verb 'translate.' The second of these is headed by the definition "to turn from one language into another." This, the editors note, is the chief current sense. The first division concerns movement from one person, place, or condition to another, especially with religious emphasis or connotation; and the third reads, "to change in form, appearance, or substance; to transmute; to transform, alter." The second definition included under the second main division is, however, the one that may interest us most: "to interpret, explain; to expound the significance of…, to express [one thing] in terms of another." This definition is prefixed by the abbreviation for 'in figurative use,' and the examples (unlike those for most of the other definitions given) date from the early seventeenth century. The short answer to the question "How can dream interpretation be translation except in a metaphorical sense?" is that it is indeed 'translation' in this metaphorical sense. But is this perhaps to skirt the interesting philosophical issue? On the contrary, I believe it points to its heart.

What the 'metaphorical' use of the word allows is precisely the right set of emphases in the consideration of Freud's account: it allows that dreams, that primary process thoughts in general, can be non-linguistic in form, and nevertheless *possess meaning*. I will return in a moment to the most provocative aspect of this claim. Here, I wish to proceed directly to the central question of my discussion: If dreams do indeed have meaning, and they are our dreams, why do they need to be *interpreted* before we can find this out? Why do our primary process thoughts *require* translation into secondary process before we can acknowledge that they are intelligible?

Freud's answer was that the *content* of dreams was dangerous to civilization – that our dreams express instinctual aggressive and sexual wishes which, were we to act on them, would destroy the social fabric. These wishes must be repressed – kept from our conscious awareness – but still allowed some form of expression, lest the endogenous instinctual energy invested in them overwhelm the individual. Hence, they are consigned to our dream-life, forced to assume shapes that allow them to pass before morality's censorious eye unrecognized.

While I think this account may indeed have merit in the ferociously bourgeois context of turn-of-the-century Vienna for whose dreamers and neurotics it was devised, as a *general* account – say, for our own rather more licentious times – it seems a little thin. My own experience suggests that some dreams are indeed about subjects that are preoccupying me but that I'd rather not *admit* are preoccupying me; but a large number of them are about – apparently – quite unthreatening matters, most mundane, a few rather more interesting. Why, then, does the mind cast them in primary process form? – for indubitably in my own case, *that* part of Freud's account seems to stand. If they don't *need* to be kept from secondary process awareness, why are they? Why do I need a secondary process translation to find out what I, myself, am thinking?

The straight answer to the question, I believe, is that I don't. Nor do any of us. At least not in the *conceptual* sense of 'need' that Freud's account was originally designed, at least in part, to underwrite. To put this another way: what Freud's account suggests – namely, that our thinking can proceed according to more than one pattern, and that the characteristics Freud grouped under the headings 'primary' and 'secondary process' do – more or less – pick out two such *logoi* – is roughly correct. Where I diverge from Freud is precisely the point at which Freud's own account stumbles in its articulation of the notion of 'the unconscious': the connection – or lack thereof – of such *logoi* to awareness. There is, I believe, no coherent argument in Freud that establishes a logically or psychologically necessary connection between consciousness and secondary process thought; nor, then, a convincing argument against the possibility of awareness and unmediated understanding of thought structured according to the *logos* of primary process. There may be physiological considerations in the case of dreams – one relatively distinct sub-class of primary process thought – which affect their role in our mental life, and our ability to remember them; but such a possibility, as I presently understand it, cannot weld those features of dreams to their *logic*.

That is: I think all, or at least many, of us are aware of primary-process-structured thought, at least from time to time. As I observed at the outset, its products marble our daily waking life in the form of slips of the tongue, and jokes – which, unlike dreams, do not tolerate much in the way of secondary process translation. They also apparently visit us when we're tired, or moved, or, often, when we are confronted with certain kinds of spatial problems whose solutions may strike us as evident but difficult to reconstruct in words. And it must be noted that we do, often, remember dreams – not just those that Freud would agree are relatively transparent, but dreams of striking imagistic power that, though difficult to relate, nevertheless haunt us for days. As I also indicated at the outset, Charles Rycroft among others has argued that primary process informs a good deal of the mental activity of conscious persons making and appreciating what, in this culture, we regard as lyric art – synchronous, allusive, densely imagistic compositions – in a range of media.[9] The processes of displacement and condensation are overt structural analogues of metaphor and synecdoche, as these function in both the literary and visual arts; and the 'mobility of cathexes' they are meant to embody echoes nothing so much as Keats's notion of 'negative capability': "when man is capable of being in uncertainties, Mysteries, doubts, without any irritable reaching after fact and reason." There appear also to be connections with the image- and rhythm-based thinking of many students of Dao and Zen: not merely their tolerance of paradox, but their embrace of it; the alleged resistance of their insights to linguistic expression; their insistence on a mode of awareness free from the domination of ego and its willing. And timelessness: again, a feature of the alert awareness cultivated in a range of meditative practices, and a characteristic of creative thought attested to by many lyric artists, from Mozart to Jorge Luis Borges. These observations underline, I believe, what Freud got essentially right: the existence of at least two broad currents of experience, one dominated by what we think of as logic, language, and the will, the other characterized by the *absence* of both ego and language, by timelessness, and by a profound sense of the extra-logical connectedness of things.

And, to return for a moment specifically to dreams, we should note that there are cultures other than our own in which dreams are understood very much as ours understands poems – as harbingers of growing wisdom or sound reasons to change one's life – and in which they – dreams – don't stand in need of the explications we require. "Ah," someone might object, "but they still often need *interpretation,* don't they, by shamans or elders, oracles of some sort? And," pressing the objection, "even you, a good Freudian as far as the metapsychology is concerned, predisposed to find your dreams intelligible, don't you, at least sometimes, find them opaque or obscure? Doesn't this show that interpretation *is* required?" Perhaps. But interpretation in what sense? Even though we read and speak the language in which a poem is written, we may have trouble understanding it: this doesn't mean, when we go to the literary critic, that what we're hoping for is a pedantic, heavy-footed prose allegorization. Often, what we need from the literary critic is simply suggestions like: "notice that the music in the line here is harsh and bunched with consonants, despite the apparent subject matter" or "see how the image of the crow is echoed here, and here, and here." Such 'interpretation' – namely, a highlighting of various resonances and juxtapositions, without a wholesale dismantling of the fundamental *logos* – is in many cases all that is required to help us grasp the meaning of a poem. – Or a film, or a work of visual art. Certainly, it is about the only kind of 'interpretation' a joke can bear and still remain a joke. It is at least possible that it *may* be all that is required in the case of dreams.

And indeed, if a roughly Freudian model of dream interpretation is correct, then it seems we should at least entertain the possibility of the dream not merely as interpretand but as interpretiens. – The dream as, in some cases, a re-structuring or translation of its own; as a raid on the articulate – language, logic, kidnapped by connectedness, a dense protean vision of the world. Proof that you've understood such expressions is not that you can translate them, or translate them back, into secondary process, but that you are left breathless with the shock of meaning –

with the recognition of 'having been gone up to,' as Wittgenstein would put it, with the sense of "several things dovetailed in [the] mind," as Keats would say.

*

Still: we do speak of the interpretation of dreams and mean by this, roughly, the process of rendering them intelligible. Let me approach the paradox of their alleged unintelligibility again, and finally, by framing that paradox metaphilosophically. Our response to the paradox so framed will be, I hope, of intrinsic interest to the discipline.

Metaphilosophically, the paradox looks like this: if, as I have just urged, Freud was right – dreams do have a *logos,* primary process does constitute a way of knowing – why has this not struck philosophers as important for the practice of their discipline? Why, for example, does A.R. Manser, writing in the *Encyclopedia of Philosophy,* claim that "Freud's doctrine of the unconscious is important for psychiatry; but he had little to say about the nature of dreams which is of interest to the philosopher"? Why, if I'm right that Freud's right, are this *logos* and its 'products' regarded as acceptable *objects* of (fringe) philosophical study – but the *logos* itself is nowhere regarded as a possible mode of philosophical reflection? If a broad range of our mental activities exhibits an identifiable logic of its own, why, as philosophers, do we not think it is a logic that can be used to find out about the world?

Because it isn't – logical?

What is a *logos,* anyway?

If we attend to Herakleitos' use, and not the letter of the word's etymology, a *logos* emerges in his work, as in the present discussion, as a coherent pattern, shaped by rules or resonances, whose integrity forms the basis of its ability to sustain meaning. However, as we noted above, primary process does not, in fact, constitute a *language*. At least, not a language like first- or second-order predicate calculus – its 'syntax' is imagistic and freely associative, not linear and fundamentally algebraic. And it is this, I think, that is at the root of our failure to accept that dreams are meaningful in the absence of secondary process reconstruction: it is a version of the claim that all meaning worthy of the name is in a narrow sense linguistic, and that apparent non-linguistic instances of meaning – gestures, facial expressions, music, pictures – are *parasitic* on linguistic meaning so understood. The claim seems to me clearly false, and I have elsewhere[10] defended the view that meaning is a phenomenon broader than, and an ontological category deeper than, language. It may even be broader and deeper than the notion of *logos* I am developing here, but it is at least that large. Freud was right, I believe, to see *grammatically unexceptional* language-use as secondary process's hallmark, but because of his additional association of secondary process with consciousness, such language-use then becomes the necessary condition of our *acknowledgement* of meaning, too. Thus, against both key tenets of his own theory, and the evidence, Freud, like many theoreticians over the last four hundred years, rolls meaning, understanding, awareness, and language together into one intra-synonymous ball. But even if we are willing to disentangle some of the threads, to entertain the existence of a *logos* that is not a language, can we make sense of the image of philosophy pursued according to its lights?

What is philosophy, anyway?

⁌ One way philosophy may be defined, I believe, is as thinking in love with clarity. But note that this is not yet to say what clarity *is*.

Philosophy is also, or in many quarters has also become, a job: an institutionalized practice, a way of participating in a globalized capitalist economy, something to do in one's waking hours to put food on the table, *technique* in a Heideggerean sense – constrained by bureaucracies, by pressures of numbers, by notions of 'professionalism' and, for these very reasons, less immune to fashion, insecurity, and greed than we might wish. And the thing is: however much we may deplore some of these aspects of philosophy's current academic instantiation, many of us feel compelled to at least partial compliance in order to have any contact with the disciplined clarities of thought with which we first fell in love. But the result, I believe, is that what was once, at the beginning of the seventeenth century, a *proposal* about the nature of philosophical clarity – that it consists in the shackling of imagination (Bacon), and the pursuit of rigorously mechanical analysis (Descartes) – has become enshrined as an obvious truth, one that we have lost the metaphilosophical appetite to question. It is a conception of clarity closely tied to other aspects of the Enlightenment – it permits an assembly-line approach to problems, and it allows the identification of *criteria* of philosophical production – thus engendering what would have struck Sokrates, though not the sophists, as a virtual oxymoron: philosophical career advancement. It is a conception of clarity that is hospitable to technologification – easily seduced by the prospect of digitalization, and by the idea that doing it by machine is doing it better. It is a concept of clarity that allows us to take seriously the idea that the good is utility, and that compassion and love are irrelevant to our ability to perceive what exists and to understand it. I do not wish, with this somewhat inflamed rhetoric, to suggest that a notion of clarity that stood these various emphases and attractions on their head would be preferable; what the rhetoric is meant to draw attention to is that we have forgotten that the question of what constitutes philosophical clarity *is* a *question*. Nor do I wish to hold up the shaggy, galumphing tossed-offedness of many dreams as the quintessence of philosophical enlightenment. I assume that were we to take seriously the idea of a primary-process-structured philosophical reflection, it would have to be primary process burnished and disciplined – in much the way secondary process is burnished and disciplined to produce what we recognize as sound argument. What I do wish to suggest, and what the rhetoric is meant to highlight, is that the reason we don't think dream-logic can constitute a genuine *logos* is political.

That is: it is because we *do* have the capacity to understand dreams that we must *legislate* that we do not, i.e., that we require them to speak the lingo of secondary process. In an interpretation, dreams are dragged into the culture of a narrow definition of the intelligible: secondary process syntax. The isolated gypsy in the Tokyo Stock Exchange being asked to explain herself is not a threat but a curiosity.

Civilization's discontent, in other words, is interpretation's self-doubt: the repressed knowledge that it *is* able to understand primary process without translation. The demand for interpretation is thus a gesture of delegitimization; and the eros of interpretation is not simply the exercise of power, but the location of meaning in a structure that creates the idea of power as 'rank in a hierarchy.' The academic apotheosis of this trend is not, as might be imagined, so-called 'analytic' philosophy — which at least suspects the existence of renegade mental activity against which it must be vigilant. It is, rather, poststructuralism — the blithe nihilism of *il n'y a pas de hors-texte* — that most profoundly exemplifies the exclusion of non-linguistic thought from consideration, and is thus most clearly symptomatic of contemporary intellectual malaise. Lyric poetry, on the other hand, emerges as profoundly subversive: it takes the coin of the realm and turns it into jewellery — braids it in its hair, sews it on its dress, shapes it into teeth.

And this, it seems to me, should interest us vastly. We're the anthropologists hereabouts. To take ourselves seriously as philosophers is to be curious about other cultures of thought — not for what we can appropriate from them for the purposes of the culture in which we were raised, but in their own right. We must *ask* if 'analytic rigour,' for example, or the history of the gradual identification of mind with text for another, is indeed synonymous with 'clear thought.'

I have elsewhere tried to make the case that neither is, arguing for the philosophical importance of lyric — a mode of thought with roots that resemble those of primary process, burnished and disciplined by the joint erotic trajectories of clarity and coherence. Rather than rehearse that discussion here, though, I would like to conclude by suggesting how primary process may be significant for a more overtly traditional understanding of philosophical activity, namely philosophy as the love of wisdom.

⁋ One of the strengths, as well as the complexities, of Freud's account of the mind is that it can itself be presented in any one of a number of theoretic models. I have concentrated in the preceding on the structural features of the two great systems he identified, but these systems may also be parsed in topographic, genetic, economic, or dynamic terms. It is the last two that shed light on *why* Freud took primary process to have the features it does. One reason, which I have been attempting to undermine, was the perceived need for a mode in which instinctually-flavoured thoughts could escape detection *as thoughts*. Another, allied in Freud's presentation with the first, was the *proximity* of primary process to 'somatic sources' of psychic energy. Primary process features an associative mobility of cathexes and a tolerance of paradox because the instinctual energies to which it gives expression are themselves highly plastic, and often contradictory. Those energies – instincts, drives – are organic or physical in origin: they swirl and pour ceaselessly out of the cells of our bodies, an expression, simply, of the fact that we are alive. Primary process thought is the point at which the mind emerges from the body, "like a mushroom out of its mycelium" as Freud puts it; and the point at which the body coalesces out of the mind. Emotions in particular – especially physically profound ones associated with instincts or instinctual reactions – are creatures of this frontier.[11] As I noted earlier, Freud maintained that mental illness is characterized by a complete divergence or total severance of the two systems. I believe such a divergence, such a severance, is the condition that the institutionalization of philosophy pushes us toward. That is: if Freud is even partly right about primary process's role as mediator of the psycho-somatic interface, and its phylogenetic openness to emotion, then what philosophy loses if it refuses the *logos* of primary process is the ability to speak to us as integrated entities, beings for whom questions about the good life must, in some measure, have to do with physical and emotional synthesis, as well as acute logical dissection. What philosophy loses if it refuses the *logos* of dreams is, above all, the intelligibility of itself as an *erotic stance* toward wisdom.

What is wisdom? Not, I think, the same thing as clarity. In my informal surveys of students, friends, and colleagues, negative definitions proliferate: "Well, it isn't cleverness. It isn't the same thing as being smart. It's sort of smarts with *depth*." What's depth? – A shrug. The dictionary lists the following as synonyms for wisdom: knowledge, enlightenment, learning, erudition – but we all know Mr Casaubon was not wise. Prudent? Perhaps. But whatever *phronesis* meant to Aristotle, for us it conjures too much the image of the successful banker. The etymology of the word 'wise' tells us that it is very old and comes from a generalized Indo-European root meaning to see or to know. Again, not much help. Well, then: how, or of whom, do we use the word? Herakleitos, albeit in translation, says: "The one, the only truly wise, does – and does not – consent to be called by the name of Zeus." The character of Sokrates in Plato's *Phaidros* caps the argument of the dialogue's second half by saying:

[*To call a man who writes with a knowledge of the truth, who can defend what he writes when challenged, and who can make the argument that his writing is of little worth*] – *to call such a man wise ... seems to me too much, and proper only for a god. To call him wisdom's lover ... would fit him better*" (278c–d).

And, of course, there is the famous example from the *Apology* where Sokrates characterizes his own wisdom as the knowledge that he did not know. These observations, it seems to me, actually dovetail in an interesting way with the negative definitions ("wisdom isn't just smarts or cleverness"); and they are pointing, I think, to something like the following: wisdom is thought conditioned by an awareness of *limits* to the systematically provable, articulable, or demonstrable. Whence this awareness? Plato, I think, correctly identified one source: on-going, long-term ravishment by beauty. The Dao hints at another: loss. And the folk tradition to a third: working with one's hands, in silence; attending, through the body, to the rhythms of the earth and one's own mortality. There are other routes. But for some time now, North American culture has worked to insulate itself against those I've mentioned: the noise, clutter, wealth, speed, and artificiality of late capitalism are as legion as the malls and monitors that are its embodiment. Little beauty in their precincts or among the clearcuts. Among our prophets a growing number urge that we are on the verge of significant culture-wide losses; but for many, the experience of what such losses might mean is relatively new. We find ourselves here because for several centuries we have refused to acknowledge limits. The institution of philosophy, along with everything else, is paying the price.

What has all this to do with dreams? I have been arguing that dream-logic, as Freud characterizes it, is also the *logos* of lyric art, of some forms of religious understanding, of pain and instincts denied cultural acknowledgement, of slips of the tongue, of jokes. And why did Wittgenstein claim to Malcolm that a serious and good philosophical work could be written that would consist entirely of the last? Because, I think, a joke of the sort he had in mind, a 'grammatical' joke, is the irrepressible reflex response of primary process to the pretensions of secondary process to know it all. In *Philosophical Investigations* III, Wittgenstein says: "why do we feel a grammatical joke to be *deep*? (And that is what the depth of philosophy is.)" Combining Freud and Wittgenstein then, we arrive at the suggestion that the *depth* of philosophy is revealed to us through our capacity for *primary process* reflection on what Wittgenstein called forms of life.

An example:

So, there were these two horses – thoroughbreds, y'know, Kentucky, white-washed stables, the smell of bluegrass hay. Anyway, this one horse is just coming back from a race, all lathered up and sweaty, and he says to the other one, "You'll never believe what happened to me today! It was just amazing! I was set for a terrible race – I dunno, I haven't placed in the last nineteen, I heard 'em talking about the glue factory in the exercise yard the other day – and on top of it all, I broke late from the gate. So there I am, *way* back in the pack coming around into the final stretch, when suddenly I hear these voices singing! There was a sort of rainbow light in the sky, and then I felt this sizzle at the tip of my tail that zinged up along my backbone – and I just shot ahead, passed everything on the outside and won by a length! Just incredible – haven't had a race like that in years."

"Well, now," says the other horse, "it's funny you should mention that, because just last week a very similar thing happened to me. You know I've been coming off this injury, it's been pretty up and down, mostly down lately, and I know they've been thinking of pulling me for the season. Like you, I broke late, and I could feel that twinge in my right fore, so I wasn't planning on making up for lost time – oh, I must've been sitting eleventh or twelfth going into the last turn – and then – it's just like you said – I heard voices singing and saw this rainbow of light and I felt a huge surge of energy right up my spine – and I shot ahead, flew past the lot, and won going away!"

And this greyhound who's been wandering up the alley between the stalls looks over and says, "You know, I couldn't help overhearing, and you're never gonna believe this, but practically the same thing happened to me. It was nearly three weeks ago. I was figurin' I was done for before they even fired the pistol – I got the burn-out, y'know – about as much interest in that f*****g rabbit as a trip to the vet. Well, anyway, I got myself in a tangle right at the start and was dead last coming into the home stretch. And then – just like you said – this rainbow o' light opened up above me. I could hear these voices singing, and I felt this tingle of electricity startin' at the tip of my tail and zippin' right up along my backbone. Whoo-ee. I tell you, I got my butt in gear then – practically jumped right over a coupla the other fellas I was in such a hurry – didn't just win, either, set a track record into the bargain. They couldn't believe it back in the chow line."

And the first horse turns to the other horse and says, "Would you get a load of that – a talking dog!"

The joke works (if it does!) because it subverts our understanding of the grammar of narrative relevance. But what does the subversion show? Not that the rhythm of expectations the story sets up is arbitrary: indeed, the joke affirms those rhythms. But it says they are *rhythms,* not theorems, of conversational etiquette; they carry the meaning of the story, but not as a fully elaborated semantic model does. The joke, if we get it, dissolves, while embracing, the distinction between form and content. It *shows* us that we often grasp semantic relevance as primary process does – as an indisseverable aspect of what we call 'form'; and *at the same time,* it shows us that this is something that no fully linguified notion of coherence as logical consistency can do. To put this another way: 'how to tell a story' is a form of life, and as such, basic to our experience of meaning. From the point of view of secondary process, such forms must remain arbitrary: why *can't* you change the subject here? – There's no convincing answer that points to anything like conceptual necessity. But the joke would not be *funny* if the form of narrative relevance *really were* arbitrary. The joke shows us we know it isn't arbitrary, but that we also know there is no secondary-process-acceptable line of argument that would establish this. To the extent this joke reveals 'the depth of philosophy,' what it reveals then is the *limits* of articulable, secondary process thought. The awareness of such limits, I have suggested, is nothing more than wisdom.

And to love wisdom in this case would not be simply to love knowledge, but to cherish the judicious discernment of the limitations of *styles* of knowing: for example, to know (in the sense of acknowledge) that we do not know (in the sense of have an articulate account).

*

We speak of the interpretation of dreams. I have argued that in practice, this amounts to more than the naming of an epistemological procedure; it also describes a culturally-specific act of marginalization. To acknowledge and cultivate the *logos* of primary process in philosophy would, I believe, lead not only to a fuller appreciation of a number of existing works of philosophy and an expansion of our conception of the discipline: it would enable, I hope, a reconnection with the roots of our discipline, and a greater integrity of thought. In the final chapter of *The Interpretation of Dreams,* Freud remarks:

There is often a passage in even the most thoroughly interpreted dream which has to be left obscure; this is because we become aware during the work of interpretation that at that point there is a tangle of dream-thoughts which cannot be unravelled and which moreover adds nothing to our knowledge of the content of the dream. This is the dream's navel, the spot where it reaches down into the unknown. The dream-thoughts to which we are led by interpretation cannot, from the nature of things, have any definite endings; they are bound to branch out in every direction into the intricate network of our world of thought.

So, too, philosophy. So, too, the gestures through which we bind, and let go of, our lives.

NOTES

1 *The Interpretation of Dreams* (hereafter ID), ch. VII, §E *passim.* James Strachey's translation appears in both *The Standard Edition of the Complete Psychological Works of Sigmund Freud* (hereafter SE), vols IV–V (London: Hogarth and the Institute of Psycho-Analysis, 1960), and *The Penguin Freud Library* (hereafter PFL), vol 4 (Harmondsworth: Penguin Books, 1991).

In what follows, I have eliminated a number of notes for the sake of readability. Scholarly references to many of the citations can be found in a version of this paper, "Freud's Metapsychology and the Culture of Philosophy," published in *Civilization and Oppression,* ed. Catherine Wilson, *Canadian Journal of Philosophy* Supplementary Volume 25 (1999), pp 211–226.

2 PFL, vol 11; SE, vol XIV.

3 PFL 11, p 171; SE XIV, p 169; my italics.

4 PFL 11, p 171; SE XIV, p 170; my italics.

5 Ibid. (Italics in original.)

6 That they are distinct need not entail that there is no overlap, nor that there are not ways of thinking that involve both — either simultaneously, or as poles of a continuum between which the thinking moves.

7 Though it was rejected by Freud as an unsatisfactory attempt to solve the problem of consciousness, its prescience may be measured by the enthusiasm that has greeted accounts such as George Edelman's. Although Edelman does not claim to be a neo-Freudian, there are numerous and significant points of comparison. See especially *Neural Darwinism: The Theory of Neuronal Group Selection* and *The Remembered Present: A Biological Theory of Consciousness* (New York: Basic Books, 1987 and 1989, respectively). See also K.H. Pribram and M.M. Gill's *Freud's "Project" Re-Assessed* (New York, Basic Books, 1976).

8 Freud's continued use of the word *cathexis* is one of the strongest indicators of the degree to which his later thought remained indebted to the model sketched in the "Project." The word signifies, here, the psychic energy with which an idea, image, or object is invested; and Freud's understanding of this phenomenon remained metaphorically, if not literally, quantitative.

Examples may help clarify his notions of displacement and condensation. According to the theory, we would speak of 'displacement' in the following sort of case: a person, unable to acknowledge childhood abuse at the hands of a parent, displaces the feelings attendant on the abuse onto a chronic disease from which the parent suffered, and hence regards the disease with a degree of terror, anger, and grief that most of us would find puzzling. We would speak of 'condensation,' on the other hand, when a person anxious about job security, on the outs with a co-worker, and under siege from a bureaucracy, dreams that a key piece of equipment keeps malfunctioning. However, it should be noted that the two do not always function independently. For example, feelings about a sequence of events — an unexpected visit by a family member, a quarrel, a disturbing insight about that person's past relations with someone else – may be focussed in or on a single apparently minor occurrence, tea staining a napkin, say. Condensation? Displacement? Arguably both.

Freud himself provides elaborations and examples in ID, ch. VI, §§ A and B, and ch. VII, § E; PFL 4, pp 753–6; SE V, pp 595–7.

9 See, for example, Charles Rycroft, "Freud and the Imagination," *The New York Review of Books,* vol 22.5 (3 April 1975), pp 26–30.

Freud himself did not write much about music, priding himself on having a tin ear. Are music and its appreciation products of primary or secondary process thought, on his scheme? A difficult question, whose answer may well be "both." To the extent that primary process is involved, however, it would have to be primary process of which we are to some degree aware.

10 *Lyric Philosophy* (University of Toronto Press, 1992).

11 Freud does not spend as much time on the metapsychological nature of emotions as one might expect. The most explicit clue occurs in "The Unconscious," §III (PFL 11, p 181; SE XIV, p. 178), where Freud writes: "The whole difference [between unconscious ideas and unconscious affects] arises from the fact that ideas are cathexes – basically of memory traces – whilst affects and emotions correspond to *processes of discharge,* the final manifestations of which are perceived as feelings" (my italics). Primary processes remain, throughout Freud's work, those which are directed towards discharge, while secondary processes are those responsible for its inhibition. See in particular ID: PFL 4, p 761, SE V, pp 601–2, and "The Unconscious," PFL 11, p 192; SE XIV, p 188.

II

Robert Bringhurst

Poetry and Thinking

*A lecture at Luther College, University of Regina,
25 January 2001*[1]

IN THE FALL OF 1930, Ludwig Wittgenstein was asked to give a title to the course he was going to teach at Cambridge University. He grunted and brooded for a time and then muttered simply *Philosophy*. Late last year, when I was asked for a title for this lecture, I was sorely tempted simply to say *Poetry*. That, if you like, is the real title. *Poetry and Thinking,* which might sound still more grand, or still more grandiose, is only the redundant explanation. Poetry *is* thinking, real thinking. And real thinking is poetry.

Herakleitos – evidently the earliest prose poet whose work survives – says something that might help us get this clear: ξυνόν ἐστι πᾶσι τὸ φρονέειν: "All things think and are linked together by thinking." Parmenides answers him in verse: τὸ γὰρ αὐτὸ νοεῖν ἔστιν τε καὶ εἶναι: "To be and to have meaning are the same." These are concise definitions of poetry and brief explanations of how it has come to exist. Poetry is not manmade; it is not pretty words; it is not something hybridized by humans on the farm of human language. Poetry is a quality or aspect of existence. It is *the thinking of things.*

Language is one of the methods we use to mime and to mirror and admire it, and for that reason poetry, as mirrored in human language, has come to be taught in the English Department. They know at least as much about poetry in the Physics and Biology departments, and in the Mathematics and Music departments, but there they always call it by different names. If they are really old-fashioned, they might even call it Truth or Beauty. If they are really up to date, they will never use such words, and the silence they put in their place is the name they use for poetry. Those who are really up to date in the English Department now and then still mention poetry. But all they mean by poetry is *poems*. Poems are the tips of the icebergs afloat on the ocean of poetry. But poetry continues to exist, maybe even to thrive, whether or not we deny or misdefine it.

The obnoxious and contrary beings called poets have been around for quite some time – about three million years, if you think that poets are restricted to the genus *Homo*; maybe closer to three hundred thousand years, if you think that they're restricted to the species *Homo sapiens*. Poetry itself has been here a lot longer – as long, I suppose, as things have been thinking and dreaming themselves, which might be as long as things have existed, or maybe somewhat longer.

Poetry, of course, has many names in many languages. Its English name comes, as you know, from Greek, from the verb ποιέω, ποιεῖν, which means to do or to make. In early Greek, ποιεῖν isn't a word used for feeble-bodied creatures sitting at desks with pencil and paper; ποιεῖν is what carpenters and ironworkers do. It's the verb the Homeric poets use to talk about making a sword or a ploughshare or building a house.

Does that imply that poetry is made by human beings? That it only exists because of us? I think, myself, that making and doing are activities we share with all the other animals and plants and with plenty of other things besides. The wind on the water makes waves, the interaction of the earth and sun and moon makes tides, sun coming and going on the water and the air makes clouds, and clouds make rain, and the rain makes rivers, and the rivers feed the lakes and other rivers and the sea from which the sun keeps making clouds, and there is plenty of poetry in that, whether or not there are any human beings here to say in iambic pentameter or rhyming alexandrines that they see it and approve.

Literature, of course, is part of culture, and culture, you may think, is something distinctive to human beings. But culture is a long ways from being a human monopoly.

There are more than 4,000 species of mammals alive at the present time, and almost 9,000 living species of birds. That is a tiny fraction – less than a tenth of one per cent – of the total number of living animal species, but virtually all of those 13,000 species of mammals and birds have something intriguing in common. They train their young. They actively define and shape their species. They have two interlocking kinds of heredity: genetic and exogenetic (inside the genome and outside the genome). They inherit from previous generations not only through the genes but through the senses and the brain, by learning skills and facts and songs and patterns of behavior. Then they keep on learning. And they teach skills and facts and songs and patterns of behavior to the younger generation in their turn.

These two kinds of heredity are as different as the hard disk and the RAM in your computer. The part that is written to the genes is like the part that is written to disk. It can easily be corrupted or destroyed, but it comes with a kind of insurance. It exists in multiple copies, in the bodies of other human beings. That's the back up: other human beings, other members of the same living species. The part that is not genetic is always at risk. That's the cultural part. As soon as you turn off the power – as soon as you pull the plug on any society, any band, any village, any tribe, any language, any family, any group of social animals – humans, wolves, moose, whales or whiskeyjacks, or any other species that trains and raises its young – as soon as you wreck its social organization, the cultural part of its heredity is torn to smithereens.

There is something unusual, though, about the culture of human beings, compared with the culture of other animals. We are unusual in the degree to which we draw not only parents but grandparents and ancestors into the educational process. The native nations of North America claim, quite justifiably, to be more cultured than colonial societies, because of the strong relationships they form between children and grandparents, and the respect they pay in general to their elders. Colonial societies, and those of the old world, though they pack their elders off to retirement communities and rest homes, claim to be more cultured than everyone else because of their obsession with old books and historical records, which extend the thread of exogenetic heredity still further.

Taking a narrow view, we can say that everything required to be a trout or shark or black spruce or mosquito is transmitted though the genes. It has to be, because these and millions of other species abandon their young as eggs or spores or seeds. But to be a winter wren or moose or black bear, or to be a human being, a standard share in the species' genetic bankroll is simply not enough. An education is required. That's culture. It isn't a luxury; it's life-support. And it certainly isn't restricted to human beings.

In the broader view, it's obvious that even for the black spruce or the trout, genetic endowment alone is inadequate. The trout needs a trout stream. The spruce needs groundwater, sunshine, clean air, and it needs the forest floor. All of us – animals, plants, bacteria and fungi – need the community we create for one another and the earth that underlies it and the sun that keeps it warm. The community we create for one another is, of course, the ecosystem. *That* is culture in the large sense. Culture in this large sense is identical with nature. It is nature *seen from the inside*. From the standpoint of any given species, this culture in the large sense – nature, the environment – is exogenetic too. It is genetically produced and genetically maintained, but not by any single species. By itself, no species can create a situation that enables it to live, much less to thrive.

About 1500 years ago, a young scholar from the east coast of China, whose name was Liú Xié, wrote a book he called *Wén xīn diāo lóng* (文心雕龍), "The Literary Mind and the Carving of Dragons." On the opening page is a sentence I have loved and pondered for some time. The sentence says:

日月 ⋯ 山川 ⋯ 此蓋道之文也
rì yuè　　shān chuān　　cǐ　gài　dào　zhī　wén　yě

This means, "sun and moon (日月), mountains and rivers (山川): these are really the *wén* (文) of *dào* (道)." *Wén* is the Chinese word for pattern, for culture, and for literature or writing. And *dào* is one of the few Chinese words most English speakers know, if only because they have heard of the Taoist masters Lǎo Zi and Zhuāng Zi (Lao Tzu and Chuang Tzu) and of Lǎo Zi's book the *Dàodé Jing* (*Tao Te Ching*). *Dào* (道) means way or path or street or road. This is not a mystical term; you see it on street signs and maps all over China. But in Chinese philosophical tradition, *dào,* the Way, suggests the natural, inevitable way. The way of hot air is to rise; the way of water is to boil when hot, freeze when cold, and run down hill when liquid; the way of the mountain goat is to climb on the cliffs and eat grass; the way of the grizzly is to eat berries and fish in the summer and to hibernate in winter. In a still more general sense, *dào* means *reality, truth* or *existence.* So what does it mean to be the *wén* of *dào*? It means to be the language and writing of being, the culture of nature, the epic poem of the world itself. The culture of nature is the culture all these other cultures are a part of, the culture of the whole which none of the parts can do without.

Sun, moon, mountains and rivers are the writing of being, the literature of what-is. Long before our species was born, the books had been written. The library was here before we were. We live in it. We can add to it, or we can try; we can also subtract from it. We can chop it down, incinerate it, strip mine it, poison it, bury it under our trash. But we didn't create it, and if we destroy it, we cannot replace it. Literature, culture, pattern aren't manmade. The culture of the Tao is not man-made, and the culture of *humans* is not man-made; it is just the human part of the culture of the whole.

When you think intensely and beautifully, something happens. That something is called poetry. If you think that way and speak at the same time, poetry gets in your mouth. If someone hears you, it gets in their ears. If you think that way and write at the same time, then poetry gets written. But poetry *exists* in any case. The question is only: are you going to take part, and if so, how?

Simone Weil wrote something once in her notebook

about the purpose of works of art, and the purpose of words: *Il leur appartient de témoigner à la manière d'un pommier en fleurs, à la manière des étoiles.*² "Their function is to testify, after the fashion of blossoming apple trees and stars." When words do what blossoming apple trees do, and what stars do, poetry is what you read or hear.

Aristotle called this process μίμησις. This has been translated as "imitation," but *participation* would be closer. It is imitation in the culturally significant sense of the word: the sense in which children imitate their elders and apprentices their masters. Μίμησις means *learning by doing*. And words, as Weil reminds us, are not just poker chips that are used for passing judgements or passing exams. Words are the tracks left by the breath of the mind as it passes across the breath of the lungs. Words are for shining, like apple blossoms, like stars, giving a sign that life is lived here too, that thought is happening here too, among the human beings, just as it is in the forest, the oceans, the mountains where no humans are around.

Some people are led to the writing of poetry – or to painting, dance or music – on the promise that it will allow them to "express themselves." Insofar as you are a part of the older, richer, larger and more knowledgeable whole we call the world, and insofar as you are a student or apprentice of that world, expressing yourself may be worth the time and trouble. But if it is really only your *self* that you are interested in, I venture to think that performing someone else's poem – reciting it or reading it aloud – is likely better medicine than writing. Poetry, like science, is a way of finding out – by trying to state perceptively and clearly – what exists and what is going on. That is too much for the self to handle. That is why, when you go to work for the poem, you give yourself away. Composing a poem is a way of leaving the self behind and getting involved in something larger.

I remember also a letter that Weil wrote from Casablanca in 1942, trying to explain why, after she'd embraced the central doctrines of Christianity, she refused to join the church. This is what she said:

Le degré de probité intellectuelle qui est obligatoire pour moi, en raison de ma vocation propre, exige que ma pensée soit indifférente à toutes les idées sans exception.... Ainsi l'eau est indifférente aux objets qui y tombent; elle ne les pèse pas; ce sont eux qui s'y pèsent eux-mêmes après un certain temps d'oscillation.[3]

The degree of intellectual probity required of me, by reason of my own vocation, demands that my thought remain indifferent to all ideas, bar none.... Water is indifferent in this way to objects that fall into it. The water does not weigh them; it is they who weigh themselves after bobbing up and down a little while.

Poetry will weigh you too, I guess, if you give yourself to poetry. But taking the measure of the self is not the same as self expression. The reason for writing poetry is that poetry knows more than those who write it. My job as a poet is to listen, not to talk. I stand here talking at the moment, but if I want to write some poetry, I have to close my eyes or leave you and go elsewhere, and be quiet enough for poetry to be heard.

Poetry is what I start to hear when I concede the world's ability to manage and to understand itself. It is the language of the world: something humans overhear if they are willing to pay attention, and something that the world will teach us to speak, if we allow the world to do so. It is the *wén* of *dào*: a music that we learn to see, to feel, to hear, to smell, and then to think, and then to answer. But not to repeat. *Mimesis* is not repetition.

One way of answering that music is to sing. Humans, like birds, are able to make songs and pass them on. Human songs, like birdsongs, are part nature and part culture: part genetic predilection, part cultural inheritance or training, part individual inflection or creation. These are the three parts of *mimesis*. If the proportion of individual creation in human song is greater than in birdsong, that's no cause for pride, though it may be very good cause for excitement. What it means is that nature and culture both are at greater risk from us than they are from birds.

Another way of answering the music of the world is, of course, by telling stories. This is the most ancient and widespread of all philosophical methods. But story, like song, is not a genre that humans invented. The story is an essential part of language, a basic part of speech, just like the sentence, only larger. Words make sentences, sentences make stories, and stories make up a still larger part of speech, called a mythology. These are essential tools of thinking. The story is just as indispensable to thinking as the sentence.

Are there are other ways to think besides in language? Of course. But perhaps a better way to say that is, there are other languages to think in: the languages of mathematics, the languages of music, languages of color, shape and gesture. Language is what something becomes when you think in it. The forest thinks in trees – and in smaller vascular plants, mosses and fungi. Life as we know it thinks, it seems, in nucleic acids. Humans often, but not always, think in sentences and stories.

People have tried to tell me that language is the source and basis of poetry. I'm pretty sure that's backwards.

Language is what thought and poetry *produce*. And stories are the fruit that language bears. You and I are stories told in ribonucleic acid. The *Iliad* is a story told in Greek. Stories are pretty ingenious at getting themselves told.

Plato, for good reason, tells his myths, his stories, through the mouth of a non-writer, Socrates. This is a link to the older tradition of narrative philosophy, now ignored in a lot of the places where philosophy is taught. If you enter into a truly oral culture, you find that almost all philosophical works are narrative. The primary way – and maybe the only way – of doing sustained and serious philosophy in an oral culture is by telling stories.

The two greatest works of Haida philosophy, for example, are *Xhuuya Qaagaangas* and the Qquuna Cycle. These happen to be among the longest and densest extant works of Haida narrative literature. Both are mythic cycles, dictated in October 1900 by a man named Skaay, who could neither read nor write, but who could think, in narrative terms, with extraordinary clarity, depth and beauty.

A myth is a particular kind of story: a story that thinks about the world and so becomes, in some inherent sense, poetic. Myth is often misconstrued as something threatened by or threatening to science, or as a kind of misinformation for which science is the cure. Myth is actually, however, an alternative kind of science; that is, an alternative kind of investigation. It is a means of understanding and elucidating the nature of the world. It aims, like science, at perceiving and expressing ultimate truths. But the hypotheses of myth are framed as stories, not equations, technical descriptions, or taxonomic rules. A myth, nonetheless, is a story so perceptive of reality that it might be rediscovered, like any law of nature, in almost any culture at almost any time. Such stories deal more often with the gods or other elemental powers than they do with human beings. Yet as soon as they are heard, they are seen to enrich human experience. That is why they are incessantly retold.

The scientist may begin an investigation by quantifying reality. The mythteller personifies it instead, and then proceeds by narrative interaction instead of computation. A myth begins with the assumption that all existents are alive: they have identities and appetites and wills, which necessarily reveal themselves in stories rather than equations. Experimental science very often gives the opposite impression, that all existents might as well be dead.

Reduced to its briefest form, a myth may look quite barren of information. *Oedipus married his mother Jocasta* or *The Raven stole the sunlight from its owner* does not in itself appear to tell us very much. But neither does $e = mc^2$, or *The fleur-de-lis is a plant of the genus Iris, of the family Iridaceae, with petaloid branches on the style*. All such statements assume a knowledge of context, and that context is always of two kinds. On one hand, the context of a myth is always another myth, just as the context of a botanical classification is always another classification. On the other hand, the context of a myth is always a world of living entities linked imperfectly but powerfully by moral obligations, while the context of a scientific statement often purports to be a purely material world, a visionless world devoid of moral concerns.

The proposition that the world is *empty of thinking* is an interesting myth in itself: one that has proven heuristically useful as well as hugely destructive. Yet it's an odd myth – and so is any other – for a thinker to believe. Myths are *theses,* not *beliefs*. In normal, healthy cultures (which are not now easy things to find, among humans or nonhumans) myths are numerous and various enough to make their literal acceptance quite unlikely. The work of the mythteller, the poet, like that of the scientist, is learning *how to think,* not deciding *what to believe.*

The parallel careers of mythology and science raise a simple question: how do we put mythology to use? What, if anything, stands in the same relation to mythology as engineering does to science? The answer is evidently literature. Literature, in other words, is to a large extent applied mythology. But literature includes modes other than the narrative, and much that passes for literature is openly concerned with the transitory, the secular, the personal, the petty, the mundane – in short, with the nonmythic. Myths are stories that investigate the nature of the world from the standpoints of the world, whereas novels, for example, more often look at questions of proprietary interest to human beings alone. These are among the reasons why myth is often glossed as "sacred story," while other kinds of stories are taken to be secular.

There is also such a thing as *social mythology,* which in its way resembles social science. Both can be traced at least to the Neolithic, and both have had a heyday since the Industrial Revolution. When humans cease to feel they are surrounded by the world, and come instead to feel that they have the world surrounded, the perspective on which mythic thought depends has been inverted. Social mythologies, framed on the assumption that humans are surrounded only by other humans, not by a real world, are the usual result. But most social mythology is no more mythological than most social science is scientific. The "myths" of racial superiority, manifest destiny, or the dictatorship of the proletariat, like the "myth" of the New World and its divinely sanctioned conquest, are less attempts to celebrate and understand the world than charters for its wholesale exploitation. These social charters bear the same relation to genuine mythology that social and behavioral engineering do to genuine science. Real myths are not manmade, any more than the laws of physics are manmade, though we rely on human beings, using human languages, to formulate and explore them.

In the fall of 1918, as you know, the German army was on manoeuvres in the Ardennes. Among the many units on that front was a meteorological team. One member of this team was a young man, 29 years old, whose civilian occupation was teaching philosophy. He was then very active in the Catholic Church but had been called, like many other academics, into military service. His military job was making periodic checks of windspeed and barometric pressure, then reporting these to senior officers, who used them to schedule attacks with poison gas. This soldier's name was Martin Heidegger. Twenty-five years later, in the midst of another war, he continued to insist that it was noble to be German and godly to die for the fatherland.

Heidegger liked myths, he liked poetic stories, just as Plato did, but he seems to have lacked Plato's suspicions. I don't believe that Heidegger ever suggests that poets be banished from anywhere. And I wonder if that has something to do with the fact that he missed the crucial difference between the social myths, the pseudomyths, of the National Socialist movement and genuine myths – those to be found, for example, in Sophocles' plays.

The centrepiece of Heidegger's *Introduction to Metaphysics,* as most of you know, is a chorus from Sophocles' *Antigone.* That play has lasted a long time – but so has the social myth of Teutonic supremacy, so perhaps longevity is no test of social value or of truth. The play, in any case, and especially the chorus Heidegger picked out, seems to me to shine some light on the distinction between social myths and real myths, or the false myths and the true. Poetry, actually, is the test. The myth of racial superiority doesn't shine like a flowering apple tree or a star. It isn't poetic. That's evidence – possibly not proof in itself, but certainly evidence – that it isn't true.

A few decades ago, when the War in Vietnam was at its height, *Antigone* seemed a very powerful and current piece of theatre to me and some of my friends. Much more recently, I've learned, it's been important to a group of Native women in Saskatchewan – and for equally good reasons. Antigone, remember, is thinking about connections and relations: about the tough coexistence of resemblances and differences. The people she's surrounded by are obsessed with homogenization and division. They want absolute distinctions between enemies and allies. Their world has shrunk from one to two. The two are "them" and "us."

In Sophocles' play, just as in Germany in 1918 and again in 1943, all the able-bodied people are in military service. There's no one left to sing in the chorus except the elders. So again and again, the old people of Thebes come out on stage and do a geriatric dance. And while they dance, they sing, and while they sing, they think. At the core of the play, sung by these elders, is the song that reappears, like a lost dream, at the centre of Heidegger's book. In Greek, it sounds like this:

> πολλὰ τὰ δεινὰ κοὐδὲν ἀνθρώπου
> δεινότερον πέλει·
> τοῦτο καὶ πολιοῦ πέραν
> πόντου χειμερίῳ νότῳ

χωρεῖ, περιβρυχίοισιν
περῶν ὑπ' οἴδμασιν, θεῶν
τε τὰν ὑπερτάταν, Γᾶν
ἄφθιτον, ἀκαμάταν ἀποτρύεται,
ἰλλομένων ἀρότρων ἔτος εἰς ἔτος,
ἱππείῳ γένει πολεύων.

κουφονόων τε φῦλον ὀρνίθων
    ἀμφιβαλὼν ἄγει
καὶ θηρῶν ἀγρίων ἔθνη
πόντου τ' εἰναλίαν φύσιν
σπείραισι δικτυοκλώστοις,
περιφραδὴς ἀνήρ· κρατεῖ
δὲ μηχαναῖς ἀγραύλου
θηρὸς ὀρεσσιβάτα, λασιαύχενά θ'
ἵππον ὀχμάζεται ἀμφὶ λόφον ζυγῷ
οὔρειόν τ' ἀκμῆτα ταῦρον.

καὶ φθέγμα καὶ ἀνεμόεν
    φρόνημα καὶ ἀστυνόμους
ὀργὰς ἐδιδάξατο καὶ δυσαύλων
πάγων ὑπαίθρεια καὶ
δύσομβρα φεύγειν βέλη
παντοπόρος· ἄπορος ἐπ' οὐδὲν ἔρχεται
τὸ μέλλον· Ἅιδα μόνον
φεῦξιν οὐκ ἐπάξεται·
νόσων δ' ἀμηχάνων φυγὰς
    ξυμπέφρασται.

σοφόν τι τὸ μηχανόεν
    τέχνας ὑπὲρ ἐλπίδ' ἔχων
τοτὲ μὲν κακόν, ἄλλοτ' ἐπ' ἐσθλὸν ἕρπει.
νόμους παρείρων χθονὸς

> θεῶν τ' ἔνορκον δίκαν
> ὑψίπολις· ἄπολις ὅτῳ τὸ μὴ καλὸν
> ξύνεστι τόλμας χάριν.
> μήτ' ἐμοὶ παρέστιος
> γένοιτο μήτ' ἴσον φρονῶν
>   ὃς τάδ' ἔρδοι.

Heidegger translated the song into German. This is one attempt to put it into English:

> *Strangeness is frequent enough, but nothing*
> *is ever as strange as a man is.*
> *For instance,*
> *out there,*
> *riding the grey-maned water,*
> *heavy weather on the southwest quarter,*
> *jarred by the sea's thunder,*
> *tacking through the bruise-blue waves.*
> *Or he paws at the eldest of goddesses,*
> *earth, as though she were made*
> *out of gifts and forgiveness,*
> *driving the plough in its circle year after year*
> *with what used to be horses.*
>
> *Birds' minds climb the air, yet he snares them,*
> *and creatures of the field.*
> *These*
> *and the flocks*
> *of the deep sea. He unfurls*
> *his folded nets for their funeral shrouds.*
> *Man the tactician.*
> *So, as you see, by his sly*
> *inventions he masters*

*his betters: the deep-throated
goats of the mountain,
and horses. His yokes ride the necks
of the tireless bulls who once haunted these hills.*

*And the sounds in his own throat
gather the breezes that rise in his mind.
He has learned how to sit on committees
and learned to build houses and barns
against blizzards and gales.
He manages all and yet manages
nothing. Nothing is closed
to the reach of his will,
and yet he has found no road out of hell.
His fate, we all know, is precisely
what he has never outwitted.*

*Wise, yes — or ingenious.
More knowledge than hope in his hand,
and evil comes out of it sometimes,
and sometimes he creeps toward nobility.
Warped on the earth's loom
and dyed in the thought of the gods,
a man should add beauty and strength to his city.
But he is no citizen whatsoever
if he is tied to the ugly by fear or by pride
or by greed or by love of disorder — or order. May no one
who does not still wonder what he is and what he does
suddenly arrive at my fireside.*

I hold the very simpleminded view that everything is related to everything else – and that every one is related to everyone else, and that every species is related to every other. The only way out of this tissue of interrelations, it seems to me, is to stop paying attention, and to substitute something else – hallucination, greed, pride or hatred, for example – for sensuous connection to the facts. I think it is not the world's task to entertain us, but ours to take an interest in the world.

I also subscribe to the view – not original with me – that the world is constructed in such a way as to be as interesting as possible. This is a deep tautology. Our minds, our brains, our hearts are grown out of the world, just as buttercups and mushrooms are. The world is us, and we are little replicas and pieces of the world. How could the world be anything other than *as interesting as possible* to us?

Yet all it takes to break that link is to try to control the world, or take it for granted, or ask it not to change or not to complain while we continue to carve it up. All it takes – and this is not, evidently, very difficult to do – is to sever the identity of poetry and thinking.

NOTES

1 Itinerant lecturers, like Baroque composers and bag ladies, chew their cud in public and recycle their ideas. This lecture, written at the request of Arthur Krentz and the suggestion of Heather Hodgson, borrows from another, commissioned in 1997 by Leslie Saxon and her colleagues in the Faculty of Humanities at the University of Victoria. It also borrows from my article "Mythology," commissioned by Bill New for his *Encyclopedia of Literature in Canada* (University of Toronto Press, forthcoming). I'm grateful for such colleagues and such friends.

2 Simone Weil, *Cahiers,* vol. 3 (Paris: Plon, 1974): 67.

3 Weil, *Attente de Dieu* (Paris: Fayard, 1966): 65.

Tim Lilburn

Going Home

I

WHEN I MOVED on to that forty acres that so changed me, minimalist hills I later discovered were sandhills, delta of an ancient river, what I eventually came to like about the place was its boniness. Even before I planted a garden, before I started cutting poplar deadfall, blow-down, for the stove we put in after two years, when I was just moving around on it, starting to be able to pick out deer trails, I liked the way the land gave almost nothing. It was so blond, friable, dry, intractable, threadbare. But at the very beginning, the first six months, the first winter, all of this frightened me – a little grass, blow-outs where there was bare sand below an overhanging thatch of juniper roots – there wasn't enough for the eye: I thought I'd starve. I remembered one of the apothegmata Merton had collected: if you don't manage to take in the genius of the place, let it say its piece through you, the place will throw you out. And I saw that these hills, these poplar islands, could just shrug me off, no problem. With some desperation, I drove myself to find a way into the good graces of this particular bit of land. I didn't have any place else to go; I couldn't manage being sent away. But I had no confidence I could learn to bed down where events had brought me.

2

I hadn't lived in Saskatchewan for almost fifteen years, though I'd been back for visits. Being here now was different: no plane back, no somewhere else. Things presented themselves differently. And I discovered that it was almost impossible for me to breathe here: everything, I realized, looking around, still in the city, that had shaped my growing up in Regina, churches, the university, sports teams, buildings downtown – the triumphalism of a prairie town – all appeared to hover a foot or so off the ground; and this hovering made me feel strangely breathless. Or sometimes it seemed as if all of it was leaning backward from this place as if it were caught in a wind of nostalgia for some old country, some metropolis, wherever the action currently was believed to be. What had been built here didn't seem to move easily in the body of the locale; this whole massive effort of civilization put together through incredible effort by European settlers and their descendents appeared tentative, seemed to have its eye on some other place, waiting for judgement; it was elsewhere. It appeared ready to move at any moment. I realized that at forty, though I had been probed by many psychologists, spent eight years in Jesuit formation, read many books, I had done nothing to educate myself to be someone who could live with facility, familiarity, where he was born. This incompetence, when I finally saw it, floored me. Then we moved on to the land, and I saw I really was in trouble.

3

We need to find our own way to take this place into our mouth; we must re-say our past in such a way that it will gather us here.

4

This place is so unlike us – all places, maybe, but this place especially: many, as a result, of our gestures toward it have been graceless: the busy program to plant forests on the plains started at Dundurn and other military bases, so that the land could look like a landscape and we could love it, the relentless use, these days, of chem-fallow. Finally we just filled it with our will, so that the land came to look tired in its heart: almost empty but crammed with human intention, sick with a sameness that came from us.

5

Between 1990 and 1999, I patrolled two pieces of land, the Moosewood Sandhills and the South Saskatchewan River between Pike Lake and Fish Creek, the hills and river section in north central Saskatchewan just where short grass prairie enters aspen parkland. And I tried to make sense of what I was doing in this endless pacing and looking, lying down and looking. I felt pulled, of course; I felt I had been assigned a post; but I could make very little sense of what I was up to. I worried a single thought for nearly ten years: how to be here? I thought that the European intellectual tradition, our form of interiority, had very little to offer someone transfixed by a question like this – Christianity, Greek philosophy construed as ur-rationalism, experimental science – ontologies that traditionally had appeared to obliterate the beckoning weirdness of specificity. None offered a quiet path into things, in none, it seemed, the abashed decorum that appeared appropriate in approaching the distant, unlike world. Only eros, a probe originating in me, that knew nothing, was empty, pressing, seemed promising – longing, loneliness for things, a nostalgia for a hyperbolic state of union which likely originated in nothing other than an attempt by desire itself to describe its own unchecked imagination. So I wrote and thought and talked, and moved not at all on my question. I read the underside of the old tradition, the whispered part, the *Phaedrus,* the *Symposium,* the *Republic,* various collections of desert apothegmata, Cassian's *Conferences, The Mystical Theology, The Divine Names, Periphyseon, The Cloud of Unknowing, Gravity and Grace,* read them in a full-tilt heterodox way, read them as the erotic masterpieces of the West: and I tried to watch what my own desire did. The three books I wrote over this period, *Moosewood Sandhills, Living in the World as if It Were Home, To the River,* were an attempt to track some sort of erotic unfolding going on at the same time in me. I am still thinking the same thought, but in another quadrant now, still walking, still homeless where I am. Desire shows more of itself, its unanticipatable meanderings.

The more I turned things over in my mind, the more the conviction grew that attention to eros seemed more promising than commitment to any ontology or to any ethics. Consanguinity or the impulse to this seemed more fecund than analytic knowing, the thing for which I had been educated to reach – and this erotic proximity, it finally dawned on me, came only through the stripping of wanting.

6

What does desire do as it unfolds? Is there necessity here? A river bed? I read Plato – the feather master – tried to read him by burrowing beneath all the interpretations, then carefully pored over the book he read for erotic instruction: the *Odyssey*. The long, watery striving in that poem, the mammoth, unparalleled affliction of the mind-bright man, the man of many turns, who knows every trick, sleepy, inventive, shimmering Odysseus, resourceful, immaculately solitary, the one who always remembers home, the untrustworthy one, the graced, rash man who becomes nothing other than his longing for home, the sleepy one, the sleepy one, his yearning materializing into a journey along the axis mundi itself – here was the paradigm for the range of what Plato wanted to say about desire, here the example that unbridled his speech. Late capitalism's nomadism, its own particular pursuit of homelessness, its sad, weary anarchy – no wonder few of us now are erotic: who could endure the full range of her yearning in this always-blunting milieu, who could inch toward it, pull off this feat of inching toward it? Everything drifts toward money's unintended telos of placelessness; we are not craning, not small, hurt by rootlessness; we are disasterously kept, "healed" of a saving disquiet – so how can we be where we are?

7

Corral, Frenchman River valley, southwestern Saskatchewan, early spring, 1999, still snow in the berry thickets along the coulee sides, a big wind out of the north west. The fence doesn't hold anything now: it's like a failed argument for the immortality of the soul: everything dies. More than a fence, it tingles with numberless pressings toward a precise sufficiency; old, it is a museum of muscled anxiety which, to calm itself, has tried to flicker into the near-invisibility of utility. The medieval strain of it – the fence, like abstract argument, has the fly-like suppleness of pure design; it needs no real weight: the force of intention, the mass of ingenuity, fix it to the earth. Like argument, too, it brings the thin consolation within the belief in the therapeutic nature of intricacy: structural complexity matches the world, a map, a discipline.

Something has been thrown massively into the fence: it is oiled with masculinity; there can be nothing of the one who made it that remained in reserve; he has crammed himself into what is made; the distance of the maker – the cool remove, the utilitarian calculation – doesn't show in his work. He isn't aloof from his tool; he's "gone bush" in this empty place, but what he's bolted into is not the strangeness of things here, but the false balm of techne. There is a pacing inside the tool.

The five strands of barbed wire are attached to large posts – which look implausibly like split-rail cedar (there is no cedar for miles and miles) and which are still rooted deeply – by lengths of still more barbed wire, one piece twisted around itself twenty times or more. Picture the hunkered, black weight of the shoulders and forearms behind this wrenching. But why use barbed wire in the first place as tie wire? Instead of clipping off his excess wire, he's drawn it back into the fence, looping it around each of his five strands, a dawdle and a decoration, a speaking of wire.

One corner post has been secured by punching long lengths of barbed wire under a heavy piece of pink granite; he's somehow dug under the stone to do this. The other three corner posts are attached to two inch thick steel rods driven deep: the maul has curled the dark metal at the end of each. Between the cedar posts, every six inches, he's wired in diamond willow branches he's collected from clumps along the stumpy, brown, Missouri-seeking river. There are at least four hundred of these twisted into the wire.

The fence, beautiful, mildly monstrous, is a mimesis of what? I cannot think the man who made it did not also make a little money. A lushness in the wire points that way. Another corral, same style, sits on an alkali flat a little further west in the valley, it, too, unused in sixty years.

Say he throws the pliers in the wagon and moves off. What sort of meal does he return to? I see a single supper, bachelor's delight, out of cans, supplemented by some quick frying. I also can imagine a meal produced intently, right on time, by a woman with red hands, lots of meat, potatoes, bread, coffee, pie. Either way, a thick, male solitude.

8

Some tasks appear endless, many-personed – the building of the Panama Canal, the space program. Some of these long tasks are now mostly interior: the Great Depression; World War I; World War II; the Holocaust; the aboriginal loss of land, culture, a way of life: these must be worked on through a number of lifetimes, turned over and over; with some of them the chill will never leave the bones. We are so recently embarked on the undertaking of learning to be in western North America, we hardly know we're engaged in it. Being autochthonic, learning to be spoken by the grass and cupped hills. And what we must learn is not geography, not an environmental ethics, not a land-benign economics, not a history, not respect, but a style that is so much ear, so attentive, it cannot step away from its listening and give a report of itself. It thus can't be taught – to attempt this would be to present a bogus norm capable only of fashioning dogmatism, some unearned conviction – but it can be participated in.

9

Desire, at its furthest stretch, intimate and outlandish, seems to have the lack of regularity, the ferality, of a strange mountain range: yield to its drift, its articulation, and it will position you in unguessable ways. Inventive, amassing, it is still easily blocked, even more easily nudged into forms that seem to resemble it but that are in fact ways of leaving it under the camouflage of apparent erotic engagement. Dogmatic conviction, wholehearted charm, keen immersion in the status quo, any form of hypertrophied certitude, philosophy of the usual sort: forms of exile from eros, "passion," ways to step from eros' momentum, to dodge its emptying, yet not feel the bite of self-betrayal.

10

Mary Oliver says the house you build is a dream-shape come to life. I built a root cellar in the late summer of 1991, when I was at my most confused with the land; I began the whole thing on little more than a whim late one afternoon when I started to dig into the south face of a low hill behind the house; I kept digging for three weeks, into the time of the earliest frosts, until I could no longer throw the dirt high enough to make it over my growing mounds. I made it down eight feet, nine feet – at around six feet I found curiously shaped stones and a curve of deer bones. I poured footings for a 7′ × 7′ room, set in lag bolts, inserted a bottom plate over them and built the walls. I had to stop often to drive into town to get books from the library to tell me what to do. I put the heaviest possible insulation into the walls and laid down a flat roof which I covered with straw bales, and then I buried the whole structure, later digging a ramp through the packed wet sand to the door. I knew the scrub land would eventually grow over the building but I got the process moving by throwing crested wheat seed on the mound; I left an opening in the roof for a length of black pipe to stick out, an air hole. I used to sleep in the buried house on hot nights through the following summer; I was looking for dreams; it was a place to wait. The root cellar was chunky, thick, thick-faced, dumb, stone-handed, intent: I thought I'd brought into the world a homunculus, thought I'd extruded a covert part of myself. I later saw it, after I'd done all the work, as some sort of listening post a distance out in the unknown terrain, the land that baffled me and the other world beside that world. God knows what I was after. I haven't seen the root cellar in years; I sometimes imagine that it's disappeared entirely, backed into the hill, fused.

II

Both ontologies and goodness have ossifying effects. Ontology points you toward intelligibilities, "presences," your imagination places in the world: the practice this generates is that of the self addressing one of the many hand puppets the imagination wears. Goodness tips naturally into rectitude, its moral narcissism; perhaps all along it was simply rectitude's finest name. So both systematizing pursuits – the one reaching for an understanding of essence, the other for an ethics – produce solipsistic practices, ways of standing apart from the world. But negative theology – where ravished desire goes when pointed toward something it can never say but can't turn from – isn't know-nothing-ism, nor is it laissez-faire desiring: erotic reach is effective only if it is toward something that arrests you, impoverishes, pulls, something that names you yet seems inarticulably strange: eros pulls you home only if it is in the gravitational field of something unassimilably beautiful. One mustn't conflate injunctions concerning practice with assertions about the nature of the world: if you bow toward the world it doesn't mean you must imagine shards of divinity inserted in it as a hidden, higher reality; in fact, to so imagine is to turn yourself away from the world as the world entirely. It is to leave it.

12

My grandfather lost his wife, Florence Densley Blaylock, in the spring of 1929, then, shortly after, the two small farms he worked in the area around Sequin School, not far from Gooseberry Lake, north east of Creelman, Saskatchewan. He moved from farm to rented farm in the early thirties, his four daughters leaving home at thirteen or fourteen to work for local families. During the harvest of 1940, he began to work for a big farmer in the Kipling area named Link; this man was good to him, and he stayed there a few years but he would not stay forever; for the rest of his life he moved around as a farm labourer: in his fifties, during the last years of the war, he was working on a ranch near Kelowna. My uncle Jack, his youngest child, told his father he was going into town sometime in the late summer of 1940, took the train into Regina instead, got drunk on cheap wine and passed out under the leaves of bolting, frost-touched rhubarb in the garden behind my mother's rooming house; he joined the army the next day, lying about his age, and later broke a leg in training in England the day before his regiment took part in the Dieppe raid; later still he fought in France and Holland. Very little else was said about this or any other family event: the stories my mother and aunts tell have an atomic sort of economy: this happened, then this, nothing more. I used to see this as reticence, but now as a sort of mild, oblique amor fati.

13

Desire can bring you to a good place, approaching paradisiac unions, if it is pulled by quintessential occurrence, fabulous, unlikely, provoking the whole of wanting, something whose power to draw will lead you to believe you remember it from before: correcting desire appears unexpectedly as nostalgia. Being utterly disarmed by something beautiful, a moral gesture, a person, can be such an occurrence: again you will seem to remember. You will *see* a surpassing thing and know you have seen it as it is; you will realize you have always known it was without parallel even if it had not always been present in memory.

14

My aunt had a lung removed shortly before Christmas this past winter; she wasn't that far from her eighty-fifth birthday, so, maybe not surprisingly, she never recovered from the procedure, though she lived a further two months. She wasn't in pain – this, apparently, was the point of the operation – but her death shocked her when it came into view. I happened to be in Edmonton that year, at the university, and was one of the few of her family in the city; I took her to see the doctor about the "spot" they'd recently discovered on her lung. I believe she thought she'd dodge this bullet, that she'd be told, after waiting more than two hours with others facing hard news, that the thing actually was an old tubercular scar. She was staggered, of course, once she learned her true state, but even as we pulled from the winter parking lot, it was obvious she was settling into herself to lift a cloudy weight.

15

We must start again learning how to be in this place, or at least I must. We begin from scraps. We should learn the names for things as a minimum – not to fulfill taxonomies but as acts of courtesy, for musical reasons, entering the gesture of decorum. Part of such naming will be being quiet, useless, broken maybe, if one is lucky: perhaps something will come toward us. Read the shit, read the deer trails. Practice an activism of forgetting the royalty of one's name, of yielding, of stepping aside. This will be like breathing through the whole body, the new, larger body of a place that might take us in.

The world, though, will stay nameless, even as we learn our names for it; and this, though it may appear to be, is not erotic failure: a sense of the distance of things has a wonderful ascetic effect: it breeds deference; it provides optimum growing conditions for admiration. Then we may be fed and taught; knowing, in the end, is being looked after. It, this farness, returns us to our sober selves by relieving us of our self-ministrations, our self-priesting assurances that all is well or somehow will be. Keep to this distance, I say to myself – without any loss of desire for the far things.

Jan Zwicky

Once Upon a Time in the West: Heidegger and the Poets

WELL, I'LL TELL YA – I been hearin a lot about that Marty Heidegger lately. Ain't been in for a while, but he used to show up pretty regular. Didn't care much for his politics, but he was the best shot with a Mannlicher-Schonauer I ever seen. What I been hearin is mostly from poets – well, an folks as read poetry, too – mostly 'bout that Primal Speech therapy he was gettin them into. Now I sure agree the world'd be a better place if we all thought it *should* be run by writers, instead of *bein* run by transnationals. My problem's with what thinkin of yourself as a poet the way *Marty* means poet does to your ability to pay attention to things, to really listen to an look at the world, see'r for how she is instead of what culture thinks she oughta be. We all like to think we're doin our bit for the search posse, an Marty sure gave the poets' egos a boost there; but if you really get what he's gettin at, it's not quite so simple as thinkin poets come up with a kinder gentler way of runnin camp. An to really get what he's gettin at you gotta go back years – hell, you could go back to before these parts was ever opened up if you wanted the whole story. But you ain't got all night, have you, so I'll try to keep it short an start with what happened when Manny Kant got wind of that strike over on Dave Hume's place.

See, Manny was smarter'n most folks. He got to thinkin about it an he realized that if Dave had found what he said he found, then all of science – leastways, science as we like to think about it, laws 'n stuff – was in trouble. If Hume'd got it right, then science couldn't be certain – that was the problem. Why, maybe you take this whiskey bottle here, an this time when you hold 'er out 'n let 'er go, instead of fallin, she flies off out the window, or up over your head. You can't *prove* to yourself before you do it what she's gonna do. Yeah – you think all them Laws of Science, they prove it. But that's just the point: how you gonna know they're *laws* an not just what science types call *statistical generalizations* – sorta summaries of the fact that a heap of things *happen* to've happened the same way? Dave Hume says that's exactly what they are, an it's only outta *habit* you think she's gonna fall on to the floor instead of doin somethin else.

But Kant, he's thinkin, "Uh oh – what if science ain't certain" an it hits him: "Wait a minute – if it's just a habit I think the bottle's gonna fall, well then that habit can be broken." So he tries to seriously think the bottle's gonna do somethin different – imagines himself holdin it out there, squeezin his eyes right up he's tryin so hard – but: he can't do it! An, he says, neither can you. Go ahead 'n try – you get serious with yourself about this, you can't do it no matter what. Well, then, it can't be no habit, can it? Still, that ol' Hume: he was right it ain't like a truth of logic or a definition – you gotta have some experience of the world before it'll hit ya. You gotta get out there an fool around with whiskey bottles some. So how come you can know it, for *certain,* but it ain't a truth of logic? Well, this was Kant's real red ribbon idea: he says it's like there's these filters in your head, like you got some sorta hard-wired circuitry. Everythin from the outside's gotta come through the filters before it gets to the inside – but the inside's where *you* is. So everythin you see, it's been sorta sorted – pre-shaped, like – before it gets to you. You can tell them filters're in there cause of you bein *certain* that everythin you see is gonna be in 3-D *an* it's gonna obey the Laws of Science. Now them Laws of Science – they ain't *laws* exactly, THOU SHALT NOT 'n all – they're more like names for ways stuff tends to hang together. So Causality, fr'instance – that's the sorta thing Manny Kant'd call a Law of Science: some stuff *causes* other stuff, it ain't just whacks of totally similar coincidences. An that's why you don't stop to ask yourself every time you're fixin to haul off 'n throw your coffee cup at the wall, "Now, this time, is it gonna head in the direction I throw it? Oh dear is it gonna hit the wall 'n make a mess?" Course it is, an Manny says you know it. Not cause the Laws of Science're like Decrees of God or somethin; we don't know nothin about God at this point. Nope, them Laws of Science, they're like the diagram fer the hard-wirin; an they ain't 'out there,' in the world, cause that circuitry's 'in here,' in your head. But they sure are certain. Ain't nothin gonna register in that ol' noggin of yours but what it's been filtered 'n set up by that hard-wirin. So *that's* why you can't break the habit of thinkin the whiskey bottle's gonna drop: you're hard-wired to see the world in causal 3-D, an lettin 'er go *causes* 'er to fall.

Then Hegel comes along. Now, ol' George was one long-winded sonnuva side-show host – history, he thought you had to do all of history all over agin before you could say "How de do" – but he finally gets his checkers all lined up an he says to Kant, "Well, y'know, Manny, this hard-wirin idea of yours, it's pretty good. I like it.

Gonna get me one too. But – where d'you think the circuitry diagram comes from? You start with that thing from Descartes, 'I think therefore I am,' you say the 'I am' bit is just totally obvious an you build your case from there. But, hell Manny, you just *stole* the circuitry diagram from Aristotle without thinkin where he got it from or if it was even what you actually needed, an if we're *really* hard-wired then the 'I am' bit's also gotta be obvious *because* of the hard-wirin, not as somethin separate that twigs you to the fact the hard-wirin's there, if ya see what I mean. Hmmm. Well, maybe you don't. I admit it's kinda tricky. What I mean is: you say there's stuff Out There 'n it comes 'in' through the filters 'n gets shaped by the circuitry. But listen, Manny – how can we actually know that? You say the unfiltered stuff comin through the filters *causes* us to have experience of filtered stuff – no input, no output, right? But ain't Cause one of the filters? So even sayin that, you're thinkin filtered. No way we can ever have any idea Whatsoever of Anythin that ain't been filtered. But if it's been filtered, it's 'in here' not Out There.

"So," George says to Manny, "so, number 1, there can't really be no 'in here' 'n 'out there,' it's *all* gotta be the same thing, an that thing is Thought, an number 2, if you think hard about why you went ahead 'n just reached for your Aristotle or why Aristotle come up with the categories you borrowed for your diagram, you'll realize it's all in the *language* you speak – whatever that happens to be. So Thought is the only stuff there is, an, even more important – *this* is the totally important thing, Manny – Thought itself is made of Language. It's made of Language."

Now I wanna rein in a minute so's we can see where we've got to. We starts with this worry about the nature of scientific laws – gotta figure out why we just can't change our minds about 'em like that – an we end up here: language is all there is. Now, c'mon. You can git your head awhirlin, all these fancy-dress ideas dancin an spoonin an you-know-what-else with each other, but if the place it gets you is there ain't no chairs 'n tables, ain't no paper you're readin this on, ain't no Interfor or spotted owls or ozone layer, ain't *nothin* 'out there' *but what we didn't say it first,* cause there ain't no 'out there' to begin with, an What Is's only what our pappies 'n our granpappies *said* – fer all of History 'n creation – well, I say "Whoa, Nellie!" I say you're willin to go along with that, you ain't never gone more'n half 'n hour with an empty belly, you ain't never seen nobody have a heart attack in fronta you or been caught out on the prairie in a thunderstorm. Now I'm not sayin our minds don't sometimes bend things outta shape, an I'm not sayin some of 'em don't look different if you come from Lapland instead of New Jersey, but I am sayin if you let either multiculturalism 'r modern metaphysics convince ya *you* (or you-'n-your-gang) are the Author of the World, you stopped payin attention to the bran in your Wheaties some time ago.

Which brings us to this fella Marty Heidegger. (Sorry, we're kinda skippin over some of the other guys who've called in at this saloon in between – but Fred Nietzsche, Ed Husserl, an them other boys, they're mostly just yellin "Set 'em up, George.") Anyways, this Heidegger fella, he comes in, has a drink or two – George is still pourin – shoots the shit a while, an then he says, "Fellas, time we called this dickin around quits. This crap about who's with what gang, do Ed's boys grind their coffee finer than Fred's, it's all a dead end. Time we talked about somethin that matters around here. Time we had ourselves a poetry readin." An he stands up on that table over there an starts chantin this stuff about gods 'n savin powers 'n the Light of Bein. Well, you can imagine. An the poets, a few who mostly'd just dropped in for a quick drink, they're goin crazy, whoopin 'n hollerin through the door for all the others t'come on in.

But the thing you gotta remember about Marty is, first, he went to Jesuit school before he got his spurs, an, more important, even though he don't usually say too much about it, him 'n George, they go a long way back. An I mean a *long* way back. So even though he's talkin about the world an the gods an stars an mountains, what he's really thinkin is: it's all language, all language, flat as a pancake, fur as the eye can see. What he means when he says, "Man is not the lord of bein's, he's the Shepherd of Bein" ain't quite "Quit drivin a loggin truck an go join the Sisters of Charity." Yeah, I mean, that's kinda a part of what he's meanin cause of the Jesuit thing 'n all, but the big part, the *main* part is: it's not that there's Things, Out There, an ya gotta take care of 'em; unh-uh; it's that human language equals Thought equals the Whole Sheebang. It's all happenin in here (except there ain't no 'in here' cause there ain't no Out There), inside (except there ain't no 'inside' cause there ain't no 'outside') the li'l ol' noggin. You're not makin it up exactly, cause Language – the hard-wirin – it's imposin what your analytic types'd call constraints. But in another sense y'are makin it up – cause there ain't nothin exists separate of your knowin it. If it weren't for us Language-speakers, wouldn't be no Bein to corral.

Now, says Marty, better you should be a poet with all this goin on than a technocrat. An I agree with you that part sounds pretty good. But you gotta ask why he says it. Turns out he says it cause he thinks technocrats *forgit* it's all language. They think there's stuff, separate from them, really Out There. An that, of course, is their Big Mistake. Yeah, they shouldn't do the calculatin, utilizin, Rhine-Valley-Hydroelectric-Project thing – but they only do it cause they don't realize the world ain't really out there; all that calculatin, utilizin stuff, it's just a *symptom* of the deeper problem. See, for Marty, the Jesuit-school boy, the Whole Sheebang's 'destinin,' by which he means followin its appointed course, by which he means whatever's happenin, however bad it might look to us, hasta, in some way, be a version of what the Whole Sheebang *wants* to do. An he's got this really complicated argument – part Greek, part Hegel, part fancy-pants German etymology – that what it *wants* to do is go 'n hide. What better way to hide than get dressed up as your exact opposite – a.k.a. the appearance that the world is Really Out There – an go hang out with the bad guys who're pushin that idea to extinction? If we really wanna unmask Big Science an show Bein for what it is, then we don't stop the technocrats calculatin, we show 'em that their calculatin is a *way* of constitutin Bein, a *way* of bein an Author of the World. An, of course, as soon as they see *that,* they're gonna wanna write a different book, a *poetry* book – all about Us, the Language-Possessors, the Greek-temple-with-a-view-of-the-sea Architects an Developers of that world class property, the House of Bein.

So my first itch about the Heidegger 'n Poets jamboree is those guys ain't noticed who's payin the rent on the hall: Marty didn't come up with mosta this stuff himself, he found it out in George's shed, an George'd borrowed it from Manny, who built it in the first place cause he was afraid of Dave Hume. Now it's true Marty's put his own decorations up, an foregroundin the 'appointed course' stuff as 'destinin' rather than Dialectic is a part of that. But it's just plain wrong to think the whole business is some bran new homestead broke with the poets in mind or that Marty filed his claim on it cause he didn't like machines. Yeah, sure, technology bugged him – but it ain't where the ideas come from, an it ain't where they're goin neither.

But shit, we all do that sometimes, forgit where stuff comes from. I ain't told ya much about Kant owin Gotty Leibnitz or Hume 'n Nick of Autrecourt, have I? An I ain't hardly mentioned René Without Whom or all the stuff Heidegger got from them medieval dudes. So maybe I'm too suspicious of hype an probably as guilty as anybody else of presentin things outta context. What I really want t'get ya thinkin about is this Role of the Poet stuff, language as the House of Bein, an poetry as Primal Speech. What Marty's stuff means is partly where it comes from – an tryin to get at that's been mostly the point of the history lesson. Like I say, when Marty tells ya "Bein's poem, just begun, is man," that ain't no metaphor. He means without us, without human language, there ain't nothin – not even Nothin.

Yeah, yeah, you say, but sayin thought is bein an language is thought, that don't mean the mushrooms an the railway tracks are *make believe*. You say they're real, alright, they're as real as it gets. It's just that their reality is, well, like the reality of everythin else – it *comes from* bein Thought. An of course it's us as is doing the Thinkin even while we're bein Thought (by Thought) ourselves. But I say all that just sounds like some kinda politics to me – either the kind where it don't matter what anyone does or says cause the Thinkin's just gonna roll on over 'em whether they keep runnin or not, or the kind where the Pawnee depends on us whities to Realize his or her True Potential. You think we really pay attention to the world or the things in it either way? I'm not sayin you *can't* think of the world like that. I know there's no way I can prove with some argument that that's not the way it is; an yeah, I even know that if I try, whatever argument I come up with's gonna Always Already be set on self-deconstruct. But that seems to me to be a problem with arguments, not a problem with the world.

I know: you're gonna say the logic's so damn obvious it's crazy to pretend there's any real alternative. We can't know nothin about stuff we don't know nothin about; an if we *know* it, it's a knowee. But there's no knowee without a knower an no knower without his or her perspective, a.k.a. axe to grind, whether that axe's communal property with a Destiny or whether it's a hackin an a hewin at random. Language just *is* the way the mind carves the world up. An the only world we got is the world as we know it. So thinkin the world exists without human language, you're gonna say, is like thinkin one side of a coin exists without t'other side. OK. But it's also so damn obvious the world *is* out there, an that we *don't* bring it into bein. So in the end we gotta choose: between the obviousness of what logic tells us an the obviousness of the world bein out there. It's not a choice most folks is real happy about makin once they get to thinkin about it. An of course even if you don't leap for logic, you gotta admit the world depends on us *now* cause we're set to finish 'er off – well, this version of 'er anyways, the bugs 'n mountains'll probably make it whatever we do. Question is whether you really believe once the seaweed 'n the clubmoss 'n the hydrological cycle's gone, some session of Speakin the Holy in an underground mall's gonna bring 'er back.

That's what I think poets are missin about Marty. Technocracy's just a symptom alright. The disease is thinkin human language creates the world. An I don't just mean the ol' Protestant pot-bangin against pride, though I probably mean that too. I mean somethin about *how* we pay attention to things. An I think we pay attention to 'em different if we think we're doin 'em a favour (like missionaries for the natives) than if we think they're out there on their own, doin just fine thank you, irregardless of us. Y'know the kinda guy who's so nice to his li'l lady – buyin 'er clothes, sendin 'er to them cookin courses, payin for the hairdresser – an then she up 'n leaves 'im anyways? Well, why's that happen, d'ya spose? He was payin lots've attention to her. But turns out it weren't the right kind – he was payin attention to her as a way of payin attention to himself, he weren't actually payin attention to *her*. *Even* if you're a poet an not a nasty imperialistic techno-patriarchal sonnuva bitch, if you think you're special because you make Bein happen, you're still gonna be attendin to stuff like it's your party, not like maybe it ain't nobody's party. Like maybe there ain't no party at all. Yeah, Marty used to get drunk with the farmers sometimes – but that's cause they were Volk an spoke German. I know I said George said Thought's made of whatever language you speak, but I was sorta tryin to give him the benefit of the doubt. George actually thought Thought was pretty much Greek an German. He thought it was sorta alive too, an growin, an whatever it looked like now was because of what had happened in Greece 'n Germany in the past. So Bein's not only Thought's not only Language – the Whole Sheebang's evolvin in the course of History, a.k.a. the Romantic version of the story of European art 'n ideas. Marty didn't ask no questions about any of that. Nineteenth-century German long-hairs talked about farmers knowin the "dampness an richness of the soil," "the loneliness of the field-path as the evenin falls," "the silent call of the earth, its quiet gift of the ripenin grain," "uncomplainin anxiety as to the certainty of bread," "the wordless joy of havin once more withstood want." Ever notice how it never rains fer two weeks on end? An how they *don't* talk about backaches an beatin your wife an malnutrition an class hatred? – So anyways, farmers bein these cool dudes, it was OK to drink with 'em. It's not cause Marty knew farmin for what it was an wasn't a snob. It's just another case of him thinkin the brand makes the cow.

Now some folks is gonna say, "Whyn't we just take the idea of the poet as someone real precious, as the Shepherd of Bein, like, without all t'other fuss 'n feathers? Poets get a bad enough rap in these parts, Shelley notwithstandin," they'll say, "they've had it with unacknowledgement. They've been pinin fer a philosophical look-in ever since Plato took it away from 'em. Why not say 'Language is the House of Bein' an mean Bein is delicate 'n sensitive 'n needs protectin; an poets, who're sposed to be good with words, can help out in this important task without any puffed up ideas that they're doin any more than holdin the door open or makin sure the plumbin's fixed. They can *care* about Bein – an Marty's gang'll make sure they get fed while they're doin it – without thinkin they're makin it happen." –Well, I spose you could say somethin like that, but point is, then you're sorta cheatin: the size of the bore on Marty's ideas about pattin poets on the back comes from them bein part of a whole philosophy, a philosophy of a big time philosopher. It's a bit like buyin a car cause it's painted green an made by a company with a big rep an not checkin to see if what's under the hood actually meets emission control standards. Other thing is, if you just buy the dessert without the main course, you're sorta treatin

Marty the way some guys treat gals: you're not lookin at the thing as she is, you're lookin at 'er for what you want 'er to be.

Don't get me wrong. It'd be dumb to think there ain't some big questions here. Like I said, whatever you decide to hang on to come hell or high water, downstream's a weird 'n scary place. If you think it's obvious the world is out there, turns out you have to give up on bein able to provide a proof fer how you know that. If you think it's obvious you gotta be able to provide a proof fer how you know stuff or you can't really call it Knowin – could be just Believin (which we know it ain't) or worse, what Dave called Habit – you end up having to say it's all happenin inside your head. Or, as George'd say, that there ain't no 'outside' of the 'inside' of your head: your head just is The World. Real problems either way. An no wigglin away from the fact that in the end the choice ain't logical, it ain't even epistemological. It's moral.

Yep, in the end no amount of arguin or analyzin's gonna tell you which way to jump. Believin it will's just another way of sayin you already bought your ticket for the Modern European Philosophy stagecoach. The logic choppin's only gonna get ya to the point where you can see you gotta choose on some other grounds. I said them grounds was moral cause basically you're decidin what sorta person you wanna be, how you wanna see your responsibilities – an decidin to ride with Marty's boys or not is just one more way of answerin the question. You're pickin the set of problems you'd rather live with: bein the front page story, or not bein able to connect some kinds of knowin with logic. Seems to me thinkin we're the front page story ain't got such a hot track record. Not that you can't think you're the front page story *an* think logic don't always get ya where ya wanna go – guess that'd be one way of describin fascism. But to give yourself no gate in the fence, to say Bein *needs* human language or it ain't gonna survive: fascism 'r no, I don't think that's gonna make for very good poets in the end. The love story of us 'n our reflection – not real catchy, is it. As for human language – no, you're right I can't prove it, but as fur as I can tell she ain't no House, she ain't even a lean-to: she's just a crust of caked mud stops us from seein what's unnerneath. Dust in the wind. Relyin on poets to use it to get us to the promised land's a bit like waitin for Nero's next fiddle tune to go platinum so's your toga won't get singed. That's why anybody, even Marty Heidegger, tells me poets is more important in the scheme of things than small-eyed horny toads or cut-leaf sage, I'm gonna ask 'em how the last chapter goes – could be comin up pretty fast – before I buy the book.

CONTRIBUTORS

Jan Zwicky's books include *Wittgenstein Elegies*, *Lyric Philosophy*, and *Songs for Relinquishing the Earth*. *Wisdom and Metaphor* will appear from Gaspereau Press in 2003.

Don McKay has published nine books of poetry, including *Birding, or desire*, *Night Field*, and *Another Gravity*. *Vis à Vis: Field Notes on Poetry and Wilderness*, published in 2001, is comprised primarily of essays.

Tim Lilburn's latest books are *To the River* (poems) and *Living in the World as if It Were Home* (essays). He teaches at St Peter's College, Muenster, Saskatchewan.

Dennis Lee lives in Toronto, where he is currently poet laureate. His recent books include *Nightwatch: New and Selected Poems* and *The Cat and the Wizard*.

Robert Bringhurst's recent books include *A Story as Sharp as a Knife: The Classical Haida Mythtellers and Their World* and *Being in Being*, a translation of all the surviving works of the 19th-century Haida mythteller Skaay of the Qquuna Qiighawaay.

Brian Bartlett's most recent poetry collection is *The Afterlife of Trees*, and he is completing *Living With Poetry*, a book of prose pieces. He has taught at Saint Mary's University in Halifax since 1990.

The text type in this book is
Monotype Garamond, based on the work
of the nonconformist punchcutter and printer
Jean Jannon (1580–1658)
of Paris and Sedan,
(Jannon's type was for a time wrongly
attributed to his predecessor Claude Garamond.)
The sanserif is *Gill Sans,* based on the designs
of another nonconformist, the lettercutter and sculptor
Eric Gill (1882–1940)
of Brighton, Ditchling and Capel-y-ffin.
The Greek is *Wilson Greek,* Matthew Carter's
meticulous digital reincarnation of a font first cut in steel
by the astronomer, teacher and typefounder
Ἀλέξανδρꝏ Wilson (1714–1786)
of St Andrews and Glasgow.
The Chinese font is *Adobe Kǎishū,*
based on Wèi and Jīn Dynasty script.
The titling face is *Simoncini Garamond,* drawn
by Francesco Simoncini of Bologna in the 1950s – and
based once again not on the work of Garamond
but on that of Jean Jannon.